Black Pearl

Living Black in Idaho

Editor: Maureen Rose

Cover design: Thom Hollis

Book design/layout: Jami Carpenter/theredpengirl.com

Visit my website: dennispattersonauthor.com

Printed in the United States of America

ISBN: 978-0-578-77242-4

Acknowledgments

To my parents: Donald Dolphus Patterson and Caroline Pearl Kitto (Runs Close to the Village) Patterson. For the best gift a child can receive — unconditional love. For always being there for us kids. For teaching us to be proud of our heritage. For teaching us to stand up for ourselves and others.

To my siblings: Donald, Judy, Lou, and Norma. For being siblings I have been and always will be proud of. For being part of the Patterson legacy.

To my children: Valderia, James, Trish, Darius, and Jasmine. For your love, encouragement, support, and good times.

To my grandchildren: Isaiah, Gavin, Janessa, Jayden, and Azlynn. For making me the proudest and happiest grandpa in the world.

To all my other family members and friends: For enriching my life.

To my beautiful wife, LaVonna: For your inspiration in making this book possible. For being the love of my life and always believing in me. I love you always and forever.

Contents

Chapter 1: The Early Years

A black Tahitian Pearl is almost as rare as a Black person in Idaho.

I WAS BORN IN IDAHO FALLS, IDAHO on April 14, 1955. I came home from the hospital to a wooden shack right next door to the first Black church in Idaho Falls — Church of God in Christ. I was the youngest of five children. My sister Norma was three years older than me; then there were my sisters Lou and Judy. The oldest was our big brother, Donald Duwayne. We had an outhouse and hauled water from a nearby well. Electricity was our only luxury. Mom nailed wooden orange crates to the wall and added 'curtains' to them and used them as cupboards. When the knotholes in the wood floors fell out, she would use the tops of tin cans to cover the holes. In the winter she would stuff rags between the wooden slats to keep the wind out. In spite of the conditions, Mom always kept our little house clean, and Dad always did his best to keep food on the table.

Mom was Native American, from South Dakota, and a member of the Sioux nation. Dad was African American, from Grand Island, Nebraska. In 1941 Dad enlisted in the Army and served his country in Europe until the end of World War II in 1945.

"Son, when I served, the troops were segregated; Blacks weren't considered brave or smart enough to be on the front lines, so I ended up driving trucks."

After Dad got out of the Army, he and Mom wanted to get married. However, since interracial marriage was against the law in

South Dakota and Nebraska, they got married in Salina, Kansas. Later that year they moved to Idaho Falls.

"I hate this godforsaken place," Mom would often say. She cried every day for the first six months. She felt lonely and isolated from her family and people. For the rest of her life the only family in Idaho would be us and Dad's relatives. As a result, our experience and racial identity was largely African American.

Dad used to tell us about the first time he came to Idaho Falls to visit his sister, Elvina Lewis. When he asked for directions to 1205 Bingham Avenue, the white person replied, "You mean Nigger hill." At the time Aunt Elvina and Uncle Aaron Lewis, along with his brother George, all lived on the twelve hundred block of Bingham. We lived on that same hill for the next few years.

I attended first through sixth grades at Whittier Elementary School halfway down N hill. I had lots of friends and only occasionally was called or heard the N word. My best friend was Mike Lewis. I was a skinny, shy little kid while he was an athletic, outgoing kid. A great advantage of being his friend was that he was usually the toughest kid in our grade plus a couple of grades above us. Mike provided me some protection from potential bullies. Overall, life was pretty good for a Black kid in Idaho.

I was eight-years-old, when on May 3, 1963, in Birmingham, Alabama, over 700 Black children walked out of their schools and marched to the city center to protest segregation. This was Dr. Martin Luther King's 'Children's March.' The police attacked them with batons, police dogs, and fire hoses. I sat in front of our small black and white TV in horror and disbelief. The tragedy of that day was seared into my consciousness.

Dad explained, "This is the way it is in America, kids; always stand up for yourself and don't let others put you down or call you the N word."

Mom said, "You also need to stand up for others if you can."

Dad represented strength and determination. Mom was kind, compassionate, and always giving. We knew Mom and Dad would always be there for us. They provided us with a foundation that would be our family legacy.

Almost four months later — on August 28, 1963 — our family huddled around the TV again. Dad and Mom wanted us kids to listen to Dr. Martin Luther King Jr. The camera showed more than 250,000 people crowded in the National Mall with Dr. King standing in front of the Lincoln Memorial. As he began speaking, the passion of his voice captured my attention even before his words resonated in my consciousness.

"I have a dream that my four little children will one day live in a nation where they will not be judged by the color of their skin, but by the content of their character."

His words touched me in a deep and profound way. At this moment Dr. King became my hero.

When I was about ten-years-old, I became aware of the Mormon church's teaching about Black people. Mormons comprised over 70 percent of Idaho Falls' population of approximately 34,000 with only about 100 Blacks. Pretty much every aspect of life was influenced by the church, including the local Boy Scouts, who were required to be priests in the Mormon faith before becoming Eagle Scouts. According to Mormon teaching, when Cain killed his brother, Abel (Genesis, chapter 4), God cursed him with black skin. Because of this curse Black boys couldn't become (Mormon) priests. Therefore, a black male, regardless of age or worthiness, could never become an Eagle Scout. As a result, I never had any interest in joining the Boy Scouts.

Brigham Young, the Mormon prophet who succeeded the original prophet Joseph Smith, once said, "You see some class of the human family that are black, uncouth, un-comely, disagreeable and low in their habits, wild, and seemingly deprived of nearly all the blessings of the intelligence that is generally bestowed upon mankind ... Cain might have been killed, and that would have put a termination to that line of human beings. This was not to be, and the Lord put a mark upon him, which is the flat nose and black skin" (LDS *Journal of Discourse*, vol. 7, 1863, p. 290).

I often tell people I grew up in the shadows of the Mormon Temple. For most of Idaho Falls the temple was a beacon of heavenly promise and spiritual fulfillment. The golden angel atop the temple shone brightly on sunny days as the river glistened its reflection. For me and other Blacks, the temple was a symbol of pain, oppression, and racism.

In 1966, Heavyweight Champion Muhammad Ali refused to be drafted into the military, citing his religious beliefs and opposition to the Vietnam War. His actions as a conscientious objector made him an icon of Black pride during the Civil Rights movement. While I admired his phenomenal fighting skills, I admired him more for his willingness to take on the U.S government for his values and beliefs. Dad was never a big fan of Ali. I think he was so proud of having served his country he couldn't understand anyone refusing to fight for his country.

"Dad, it's not that Ali doesn't love his country; he's simply following his beliefs," I explained.

It was ten days before my thirteenth birthday when Dr. Martin Luther King Jr. was assassinated in Memphis, Tennessee. I remember the scenes on TV of people around the world crying. In our little house in Idaho Falls, we were crying, too. It was almost as though a part of me was missing. Dr. King represented so much hope and now things seemed hopeless. I learned that the previous night Dr. King had delivered his 'I've Been to the Mountaintop' speech where he said, "Like anybody, I would like to live a long life. Longevity has its place. But I'm not concerned about that now. I just want to do God's will. And he's allowed me to go up on the mountain. And I've looked over. And I've seen the Promised Land. I may not get there with you. But I want you to know tonight, that we, as a people, will get to the promised land!"

This speech was given at the Mason Temple, Church of God in Christ, in Memphis. This happened to be the headquarters of our church, now pastored by my uncle, Aaron Lewis.

Although I wasn't a particularly good athlete, I loved watching sports. The 1968 Olympics were held in Mexico City, Mexico. My favorite event was track and field, and I used to dream about how cool it would be to win a gold medal. The idea of standing on the medal stand for all the world to see was beyond imagination. On October 16, I watched the award ceremony for the 200 m race. I was so happy to see two Americans, both Black, on the medal stand. Tommie Smith had won the gold and John Carlos had won the bronze. As the national anthem began, both raised a black-gloved fist and kept their hands raised and heads bowed until the anthem had finished. The fist salute was a symbol of Black power and human rights.

While most of white America was horrified, I felt an overwhelming sense of pride. I was proud to be Black and proud of them for the courage and bravery they displayed.

Dad said, "Kids, this day will be remembered for a long time, but I'm afraid for them when they come back to America."

I got a small sense of what Dad meant when I went to school the next day.

"Did you hear what those N's did last night at the Olympics?"

"My parents say, they should just send them back where they came from."

I wanted to say something, but instead I pretended I didn't hear what I heard. One day, I would be brave enough to stand up and speak out, but today wasn't the day.

Chapter 2: Time of Growth

IN 1970, my father was elected vice president of the Idaho Falls Laborers Union. One of my proudest moments was when Dad came home from a union meeting.

"Pearl, I'm going to a leadership conference in Florida."

"Honey, I'm so proud of you. Hey, kids, did you hear that?"

I had heard it and yes, I was over-the-top proud. We went with Mom to take Dad to the airport. He was taking his very first airplane ride. Our dad, who had to drop out of school in the tenth grade to help take care of his family, was making history as one of the first Blacks in a leadership position in Idaho Falls.

At the age of seventeen, I was hired by the Idaho National Laboratory (INL) for the summer as a laborer. The INL is a government facility managed and operated then by Aerojet Inc. It was under the purview of the U.S. Department of Energy, Idaho Operations Office (DOE-ID). At the time it was called the National Reactor Testing Station. The nuclear test reactors were located at a remote site forty-five miles west of Idaho Falls. The INL was one of the largest employers in the state and the place where most everyone wanted to work, largely because of the good pay.

The person coordinating the summer hire program happened to be Black and coincidentally was dating my sister Lou. Bill Swift had been hired as a human resource analyst in 1970, having just graduated from Fort Valley College, Atlanta, Georgia. This time period was the beginning of Affirmative Action and Equal Employment (AA/EEO). AA/EEO was a set of laws and policies intended to end and correct the effects of discrimination. In the early years it included quotas that required government contractors to take specific actions to ensure minorities were represented in the workforce.

This was my first job and my first experience with people of many different races. There were Blacks from Compton, California; Chicago, Illinois; Pocatello, Idaho; Native Americans from Fort Hall, Idaho; Japanese Americans from Idaho Falls, and Hispanics from Blackfoot, Idaho. It was truly a rainbow of peoples. Of course, the majority of our co-workers were white. We all worked together well and developed many friendships. We minorities even joked with our white counterparts that 'race has its privileges.'

My junior year in high school, the English teacher gave the class a three-page writing assignment: "What does the Declaration of Independence mean to you?" After a few days of contemplation and reflection, I wrote a one-page response noting the speech Frederick Douglas gave on July 5, 1852. Douglas spoke about the values expressed in the Declaration was an offense to Black people because of the cruelty and oppression they suffered as a result of slavery. I got an A on my paper.

I graduated from Skyline High School in 1973. Overall, my high school days were good. I only heard the N word a few times. I did well in school and had a few close friends. There were only two other Blacks. One was my cousin, Mary Lewis, and the other my friend since kindergarten, Mike Lewis.

A close friend was a white kid from my neighborhood, Craig Wilkie. When I first visited his home, a couple of little boys ran through the living room. All I could hear was the N word as one chased the other. Craig's dad yelled at the kid and the mom apologized. Although our friendship got off to a rocky start, the Wilkies treated me as family and our friendship would be one for life.

Chapter 3: New Experiences

I BEGAN COLLEGE the fall semester 1973 at Idaho State University. About twenty students were in the dorm common area watching NFL football; I was the only Black. The Pittsburgh Steelers backup quarterback was Joe Gilliam. Joe was only the second Black quarterback to play in the NFL. When he threw an errant pass, someone yelled out, f__g *N* word.

"What did you say?" I yelled in response.

Dead silence.

After a few seconds, students began cheering again, as though nothing had happened. I quietly got up and left the room.

My family took a trip to Grand Island, Nebraska for a funeral in 1974. On a Sunday evening my cousin, John Lewis, and I decided to take a drive around town to see the sights. While stopped at a stop light I noticed a police car behind us. I knew I had done nothing wrong and my driving was perfect. Nonetheless, I was scared being in a strange nearly all white town. As I pulled off, the siren blared and I saw the blinking lights on the police car. The officer came to the car and asked for my license and John's license.

"Officer, why do you want his license and why did you stop us?"

He responded, "Don't worry about it, just do what you're told."

I asked again and got the same response. He told me to sit there until he came back. Within a few minutes we were surrounded by three more police cars and the officers had their guns drawn. My heart pounded, my mind raced, and I feared this might be my last moment of life.

When the officer came back to my window, in my most polite voice I asked, "What's going on, Officer?"

"You were being a smartass and not being cooperative; I thought you were a threat."

The other officers put their guns away and after the officer ran our licenses, he let us go without even as much as an apology.

The summer of 1974 I was rehired by the INL as a laborer. I continued to enjoy the diversity and camaraderie of my fellow workers. For the next few years, I would return to college and work at the INL during the summer. My last summer working as a laborer was 1978.

I was assigned the task of using a pick and shovel to refill a large hole that had been dug the previous fall. The temperature was in the nineties and the rock pile barely moved when I swung the pick. By noon I was exhausted and had made little progress. After lunch, my foreman, Dave, stopped by. His eyes were wide and the veins in his forehead were bulging.

"What the hell have you been doing all day? You should have already filled in the hole. If you don't want to work you can catch the next bus home."

I was appalled to be approached in such a disrespectful way. I knew I was working hard and had received good performance reviews all the past summers. For the rest of the afternoon I got angrier and angrier. By the end of the day I had decided I was going to stand up and speak out. I walked into Dave's office.

"Hey, Dave, I don't like how you disrespected me. If you feel I deserve to be fired then go ahead and fire me now."

"Oh, I'm sorry, Dennis, I didn't mean anything. Yeah, you're right; you have done a good job."

For the rest of the summer I continued to work hard and I had no more problems with Dave. In fact, at times it seemed Dave went out of his way to make sure I didn't hold a grudge against him.

June 9, 1978, signaled an important and momentous change for the Mormon church. The Mormon prophet, Spencer W. Kimble, had a 'revelation.' According to Mormon teaching, a prophet is "one designated by God to be his spokesperson." Accordingly, God must have decided Blacks were no longer cursed and upon becoming twelve Black males could now enter the priesthood. For me, it seemed like the church had simply acquiesced to public and legal pressure. It had nothing to do with God speaking to anyone; it was about the church recognizing that racism was no longer being tolerated in our country.

I was friends with some returning missionaries who were so excited this time had come. However, they told me the feeling was not universal in the church. They related that they had heard comments such as, "Oh my goodness, I can't imagine having to sit next to a Negro and praying during service."

Chapter 4: Now, Real Life Begins

I GRADUATED FROM IDAHO STATE UNIVERSITY in December 1978 with a bachelor's degree in Business Administration. I was the first native Idaho Falls African American to graduate from college. The local newspaper ran my picture, one with my giant Afro. Reading the article, Mom said, "I'm so proud of you, Son; I know you're going to accomplish great things in your life."

I'm told Dad went around town bragging how his youngest had graduated college. My siblings kidded me about how my ego was as big as my Afro, but I knew they were proud of their little brother.

I immediately began applying for jobs at the INL. I was certain I would be hired because of my years of work as a summer hire and receiving positive performance reviews. However, I received no response to my inquiries.

With no success at gaining employment at the INL, I applied and was hired by the retailer Grand Central as a manager trainee. A couple of weeks after being hired, I was invited to play tennis with a few of the other managers. After the match, the security manager said, "Well, I need to get back to work to catch some Ngrs."

I immediately ran up to the net. "What did you just say?"

His face turned beet red. "What?"

"You know exactly what you said."

"Hey, man, I'm sorry, I didn't mean anything by it. In fact, my wife and I would love to invite you to dinner."

I got in his face. "Look, I don't want to come to dinner and if I ever hear that word again, it's going to be me and you."

In spite of this rocky beginning, I went on to be promoted to personnel manager. This afforded me the opportunity to hire minorities, inclusive of a couple of Blacks. I was proud to be able to make a difference in the lives of others.

I began my professional career at the INL August 1980 as a business administrator. At the time the laboratory was managed and operated by EG&G Idaho. I performed document control and configuration management services for the engineering department of the Loss of Fluid Test Facility (LOFT). To my surprise, my manager was Mormon as were many of my co-workers. It was sometimes uncomfortable listening to all the stories about their children going on Mormon missions and other church happenings. Nonetheless, I was treated well and became good friends with several of my colleagues. My boss, Bert Freed, and I would become friends for a lifetime.

After seven years of success and excellent performance, I received a notice of reduction in force. The LOFT project was coming to a close and my position was one of those being eliminated. For the next few months, I unsuccessfully applied for jobs within the laboratory. I asked a human resource person what could be keeping me from getting interviews.

"You need to review your personnel file to make sure something isn't in there that could cause a manager to be reluctant to interview you."

As I went page by page through the file, my jaw dropped. I was looking at my performance appraisal for my last summer employment in 1978. It was signed by Dave, the foreman, who had threatened to fire me, but then apologized after I confronted him.

'Not recommended for rehire,' was written in bold. 'Militant' was also written in bold.

It seemed to me that Dave had exacted his revenge for me standing up for myself. I immediately made some calls to see if he was still with the company. I gasped when the person informed me, "Dennis, Dave was killed a couple of years ago in a gas explosion at his home." Although I was extremely upset about his vengeful action, I was saddened by news of his death. No one deserved such a horrific end to their life.

With only a few weeks before being laid off I interviewed for a position for which I was highly qualified. A few days after the interview, I got a letter in the company mail. The letter thanked me for interviewing, but said I wasn't qualified for the job. Knowing this wasn't true, I filed a complaint with the company EEO manager, Frank Sanchez. Frank arranged for me to have a second interview with the same manager.

At the end of the interview the manager said, "Dennis, I think you are overqualified for this position." By some miraculous happening, in two short weeks I had gone from not qualified to overqualified.

Later I learned they hired a white female from outside the laboratory who had no college degree and no relevant experience. I went back and told Frank what had happened. He obviously recognized he needed to do something. A few days later he arranged for me to interview for a job one level above my current position.

I was excited about the possibility of a promotion. The interviewing manager was Tony Allen. He impressed me as a good leader and a person who would give me an opportunity to succeed. When I left his office, I was confident I would receive a job offer. Sure enough, a few days later human resources called, "Mr. Allen would like to offer you the job."

"Great," I replied.

"Well, there is one problem; he decided you don't have the

experience to qualify for the level the job was posted. So, the position has been downgraded one level."

"You got to be kidding me," I responded. I asked if I could speak with Mr. Allen.

Later when I met with him, I told him I was really disappointed and I wasn't comfortable accepting the job given the situation. He explained there were a couple of areas that I didn't have the depth of experience he desired, but he offered the following compromise: "Dennis, you do the job for six months and show me what you are capable of and I promise to promote you if you are successful."

I accepted his offer and we parted with a firm handshake.

Six months later, true to his word, Tony promoted me. This one experience formed a bond between us that would never be broken. He became my friend and mentor.

Chapter 5: Romance and Family

ON A BEAUTIFUL SUMMER DAY in 1987 I was having lunch in the INL cafeteria. "Dennis, I'd like to introduce you to Monica Smith," said a female colleague. Apparently, she thought it would be a good idea to introduce single Black people to each other. Whatever her thinking, I was more than pleased to meet an attractive young lady. It wasn't necessarily love at first sight, but there was a connection. We were soon dating and getting to know each other. She told me she was from Berkeley, California, and loved it there. She had two sisters; older sister Michelle was an MD, and her younger sister, Myra, was attending UC Berkeley. I was duly impressed.

"So, Monica, how did you come to work at the INL?" I asked.

"Having graduated with an engineering degree from San Francisco State, I put out resumes all over the country, and INL was the first to respond."

"How do you like it here?"

"I was so scared when I got here. All I knew about Idaho was it was headquarters for the Aryan Nation, and it was mostly Mormon." Her going from one of the most diverse and liberal cities in America to one of the most white and conservative cities created fear and anxiety. She had been hired by INL as a nuclear reactor operator. She was the first Black nuclear reactor operator at the INL.

In fact, she was one of the first Black female nuclear operators in the nation. Working in an all-white, all male environment was a daunting undertaking. Additionally, the work place was dominated by ex-Navy personnel who had little-to-no experience working with females or Blacks. Monica would tell me of the racist and sexists remarks that made her life miserable. We often discussed going to the EEO office, but she always worried it might make matters worse if her management found out she had reported her colleagues of harassment or discrimination. Monica decided to try to make the best of a difficult situation.

***

Mom had always taught us kids to be proud of our Native American heritage. Mom's maiden name was Kitto and her mother's name was Nancy Runs Close to the Village. Mom could only speak a little of her native tongue but she understood it quite well. The summer of 1988, the first-ever family reunion on Mom's side of the family was held on the Santee Sioux Reservation in South Dakota. Upon arriving, we discovered the camp area was filled with a mix of traditional Native American teepees, campers, fifth wheels, and motor homes.

There were at least a couple of hundred people. One of the first things I noticed was that everyone treated us as family, even though we had never met. The diversity in our family surprised me: there were Blacks, whites, Hispanics, Asian Americans, Pacific Islanders, and others.

The most special moment for Mom was being reunited with her niece, Merri Jo. Merri Jo's parents had died when she was just a toddler. Mom and Dad had wanted to adopt her but because they already had five kids and were poor, the state wouldn't allow the adoption. Now some thirty years later they were together again. Mom cried tears of joy mixed with regret as she hugged her long-lost niece.

The Shawl Dance is one the Native American traditions. The Native drums played as we danced with the shawls draped around our shoulders and our arms spread out. While I did my best, my efforts paled considerably when compared to the amazing dancers who had lived and breathed our culture since birth. For the four days we were there, we were totally immersed in our heritage.

Near the end of the family reunion was the traditional smoking of a long pipe. The oldest child in each family would represent that family. As such, our big brother had the honor. It was my understanding that the long pipe contained peyote. We siblings have forever teased him, because he was a minister and had never even smoked a cigarette. But there he was smoking a pipe. Of course, he always told us he didn't inhale.

***

The sun was shining, with a pale blue sky and billowing white clouds. It was August 1989, and I was dressed in a grey tuxedo. From an early age I dreamed of being married and having a family. At an age when many of my friends had teenaged children, I was now ready to say "I do." My brother stood there smiling, ready to perform the ceremony. Monica's two sisters, Myra and Michelle, beamed. My best man, Mike Lewis, and friend, Darnell Evans, stood next to me. Nephew Julian was the ring bearer, followed by niece Dezer-Rae, the flower girl. Monica looked beautiful coming down the aisle. We looked into each other's eyes as we exchanged our vows. Walking back down the aisle, I saw the faces and smiles of family and friends. Mom and Dad nodded with approval. I could see the happiness in their eyes. As we drove off in a black limousine, I knew life was good and getting better. Our honeymoon in Hawaii was all, and more than we had hoped.

Chapter 6: Struggles and Joy

IN EARLY 1990 a colleague and friend, Jimm Snoddy, began discussions with several Black employees, including me. Jim observed that there wasn't a single Black manager at INL despite there being thousands of employees. Soon, we began holding meetings. We discussed the lack of Blacks in management, the fact there were less than twenty Blacks at the INL, and the seemingly lack of interest in recruiting Blacks. We decided to form a coalition to bring our concerns to the attention of senior management. The name we chose for our group was the Black Awareness Committee (BAC). The BAC included Jimm Snoddy, Bill Swift, Darnell Evans, Americus John-Lewis (AJ), a few other Blacks, and me. The BAC formed an alliance with the EEO manager, Frank Sanchez. Within the year, we were meeting with senior management including the vice president, Jim Okeson, and general manager, Jim Zane. The BAC was able to achieve a small measure of influence to improve diversity and lay the groundwork for Blacks being a part of management at INL.

***

On June 9, 1991, joy filled the hospital room as Monica and I welcomed our first-born son, Darius Dennis Patterson. My lifelong dream of being a father had been fulfilled. He was a beautiful little boy with jet black hair. As I held him in my arms and looked out the window, I imagined the limitless future that lay before him. I heard his mom say, "Little son, we are going to give you the best life possible." We took him home to our newly built Tudor style home in what would be our home for the next sixteen years.

In the fall, my manager and mentor, Tony Allen, assigned me to the position of Technical Lead. In this position I would supervise seven employees. While not a manager position, this would be a stepping stone for my future. Tony also assisted me in enrolling into the recently instituted Unit Manager Development Program. This program was a set of courses designed to provide an understanding of the multiple functions of the laboratory. This included human resources, safety and health, finance, compliance, and applicable policies and procedures. I completed the courses with a 95 percent average. My intent was to prepare myself to be the best candidate for any upcoming manager positions.

***

As winter approached, Monica came home from work with a sadness that consumed her face. "Dennis, I made a mistake at work and I hear I might be fired." She went on to explain that she knew of white males who had made the same mistake, but nothing happened to them. Based on this information, we contacted the EEO manager and informed him of Monica's concern that she might be treated differently than her white colleagues.

Two weeks later, Monica and I attended a meeting with management, Don Sherick, EEO; Frank Sanchez; and Legal, Dennis Love. Sherick began, "Monica, you are suspended from work without pay for twenty days, effective immediately, and a discipline letter will be placed in your file."

Dennis Love added, "There was no discrimination; we have documented that white employees have been given similar discipline for the same infraction."

On the way home Monica said, "Honey, I know they're lying. If anyone had been given time off without pay, everyone would have known about it."

Monica filed a discrimination complaint with the Idaho Human Rights Commission (IHRC) in Boise, Idaho. We also retained an attorney from Pocatello, Idaho. All the Idaho Falls attorneys we contacted wanted nothing to do with taking on one of the largest employers in the State.

In a few weeks we received a letter from the IHRC. It included the written response from the INL. INL provided the names of three white males who made the same mistake and were allegedly suspended without pay. As it happened, part of my job duties included analyzing budget reports. I was able to review the time off without pay reports for the department where the three white males worked. There were no employees in that department who had received time off.

This information proved beyond doubt that INL was guilty of discrimination and had provided false data to the IHRC. The INL was ordered by the IHRC to reimburse the twenty days' pay, clean up Monica's personnel file, and recommended she be reassigned as an engineer. The IHRC did not require the INL to reimburse us for legal fees. As a result, we had to pay thousands of dollars for this egregiously wrong experience. Besides, nothing could compensate Monica for the pain and duress caused by this horrific experience. This would follow and haunt Monica for the rest of her life.

Chapter 7: Mexicans and Negroes

"UPSCALE NEIGHBORHOOD OPPOSES AFFORDABLE Neighborhood," was the headline of the April 2, 1993, *Post Register.* I was sitting in my breakfast nook reading the newspaper. First, I had no idea I lived in an 'upscale' neighborhood. Secondly, I wasn't aware that a proposed affordable neighborhood was to be built near ours. As I read further, I saw the following quote from a well-known local artist, Werner Gisin: "Mexicans, Negroes, and white negroes would move in Westridge." He said it would be "like a box where rats come in and out."

I was so outraged that I immediately looked up his number and dialed.

"Monica, I'm going to tell him he's a racist and I can't wait to meet him face to face." Fortunately, no one answered the phone. Adding to my dismay, I learned that 135 of our neighbors had met at our local elementary school to voice opposition to the affordable housing proposal.

A public forum was convened by the City Council. When they opened it up to public comment I spoke. "As the head of the only Black family in Mill Run, I am hurt and angry about the racist remarks by Gisin, and disappointed by the response from my neighbors. People have a right to affordable homes and we should not look down on those of lesser means." I also wrote a letter to the newspaper advocating for the proposed neighborhood and speaking out against racism.

A subsequent article in the *Post Register* referred to the fact that a local restaurant prominently displayed Gisin's paintings. The restaurant's owner decided to remove a plaque with Gisin's name, "because they didn't want people thinking they shared his views," but left the pictures up.

This ugly story had a beautiful ending. The affordable neighborhood was built and one of the first homeowners was Black. The father was a friend and a minister at our church. His family represented what is best about America and at the same time, Werner Gisin's worst nightmare.

Chapter 8: Fighting the Good Fight

SPRING 1993, Bishop Nathaniel Jones Jr. from Barstow, California, installed my big brother as the pastor of the church we attended. Mom and Dad sat on the front row as their first-born son was conferred, "Pastor of Community Church of God in Christ." His wife, Euranius, could hardly contain her joy. Sisters Norma, Lou, and Judy sat together right behind Euranius. I sat quietly in the back with Monica and Darius, remembering my brother's journey to this special moment. He would always minister and be guided by Ephesians 4:3: "Endeavoring to keep unity of the Spirit in the bond of peace."

***

That summer my good friend, Americus John Lewis (AJ), was voted president of the local National Association for the Advancement of Colored People (NAACP). Late one evening he called.

"Dennis, I'd like you to be the Legal Redress Officer for the NAACP."

"Umm, I don't know; let me talk to Monica and I'll let you know."

"Honey, I think you'd be great at it, you should do it."

Well, AJ and I made a great team. AJ was a gentle giant with a passion for doing the right thing. He stood six feet, nine inches and weighed about 275 pounds. As Legal Redress Officer, I assisted AJ with investigating and resolving complaints of racism and discrimination.

One of the notable complaints we received was from a mixed-race couple, husband Black and wife white. Passing through Idaho Falls on vacation, they stopped at one of our finer restaurants along the river. According to the complaint, they checked in with the hostess and were told a table would be available in just a few minutes. While waiting they observed white couples enter and be immediately seated. After about twenty minutes, they were told, "It's really busy tonight, you might want to go to a restaurant down the way."

During my investigation of this complaint I spoke to a colleague who worked part-time as a server at this restaurant. He told me, "Dennis, this happens all the time; the server working that night refuses to serve tables with minorities."

AJ and I set up an appointment to meet with the manager. "Hey guys, I don't know anything about this," he said.

I responded, "Maybe so, but I've spoken to one of your servers who told me it's well known by other servers."

The manager promised to follow-up and take necessary actions. We later learned the server had been fired and diversity training was instituted for the staff.

Another complaint alleged the husband of a daycare operator regularly used the N word around the kids and parents. Again, I spoke to an INL colleague who happened to know the husband. He told me the person used "the N word like it's a vowel."

AJ set up a meeting to speak with the white female owner. We had barely sat down when she pulled out a framed picture of herself with Eric Dickerson, a Black all-pro NFL running back. I believed in her mind this proved she wasn't a racist.

My experience has been that it is common for white people to refer to 'my black friend' as a way to defend themselves of being discriminatory or racist.

I related that my information indicated her husband routinely used the N word. "Well, he might use it occasionally, but he's never said it around the kids." Since AJ and I had no proof if that was true, we simply told her we'd return if we heard more complaints. The following year the daycare went out of business.

A house directly behind mine was for sale by the owner. I didn't know the people, but they never seemed particularly friendly. AJ received a complaint from another mixed-race couple. They alleged that when they met with the owner, they were told the sale price had gone up twenty thousand dollar from the list price. They told AJ, "We were outraged, but didn't know what to do or say." AJ asked them if they wanted NAACP to investigate; they declined. They just wanted someone to know what happened to them.

Chapter 9: Joy and Strife

THANKSGIVING was only a few weeks away, but Monica's and my thoughts were on the upcoming birth of our second child. We had already picked out her name after watching Disney's *Aladdin.* Our baby girl was going to be our Princess Jasmine. Joy filled the hospital room as Monica and I welcomed our amazingly beautiful little girl into the world and into our lives. Her gorgeous brown eyes and curly black hair melted our hearts. As Jasmine cuddled next to her mommy's face, we counted her little fingers: 1, 2, 3, 4, 5, 6, 7, 8, 9, 10 ... 11.

"Eleven!" exclaimed Monica.

The doctor smiled and said, "Everything's fine; we'll just tie a string around (the extra finger) and it will fall off in a couple of days."

I picked up Jasmine and carried her to the window like I had done with Darius. I knew Jasmine Monique's life would be filled with wonderment.

***

Right before Christmas I applied for a managerial position for which I was exceptionally qualified. Returning to work after the Christmas holidays I discovered the job had been filled without any interviews being conducted.

"How could this be?" I said aloud as I sat at my desk. I had a business degree, completed manager training with high marks, excellent appraisals, and thirteen years of experience. I decided to make some informal inquiries with a few of my colleagues. I discovered that the person selected had no college, no manager training, and limited experience.

After talking to Monica and AJ, I decided to contact Frank Sanchez, EEO manager.

"Frank, I'm concerned there could be discrimination."

"Dennis, I can see why you're concerned; how about I set up a meeting with the hiring manager so we can talk it out."

"Sure, Frank, but this doesn't look good."

In the meeting, the manager, Bob Scott, began by explaining that after he posted the job, he realized he already knew who he wanted in the position. It was somebody already working for him so he just promoted her.

"It would have been a waste of everyone's time to conduct interviews," he added.

"So, Bob, what's her name?" I asked.

He responded, "Lori."

"Bob, how do her qualifications compare to mine?"

Bob's face went fire red and his eyes bulged. Standing up and pointing his finger at me he screamed, "I'm in your face, man." After he slammed the door, the pictures on the wall rattled.

I took a deep breath and looked over at Frank. Frank threw his pen on the desk, looked back at me, and said, "Well, I guess we'll see if the bear shits in the woods." I had no idea what this meant, but I was anxious to find out.

About ten months prior to this unfortunate event, I had been reassigned to a senior manager, Dennis Keiser. In this brief time Dennis and I had developed a close working relationship. On the day of the threat from Bob, Dennis was in Washington D.C. When notified of what had occurred, he cut his trip short and returned immediately to Idaho Falls. I already respected Dennis, but this made me respect him even more.

A few days later, Bob was removed from his manager position and the job was reposted. Unfortunately, the manager who replaced Bob, Phil McDonald, had a reputation for being intimidating, threatening, and a bully. In fact, Bill Swift, my brother-in-law, had been cursed out by him. Bill told me he was close to going to his office and confronting him. Nonetheless, I immediately applied for the job and was interviewed.

Two weeks later, Phil called me at home. "Dennis, you've been selected for the job; do you accept?"

"Well, that depends; how much raise will I get?"

He responded brusquely, "$43 a month."

"Well, Phil, I'll need to think about it."

"Fine, but that's all you're going to get."

I subsequently met with the vice president, explained the circumstances, and asked that he consider increasing the raise. The following week, I received a call from Human Resources.

"Dennis, management would like to offer you the manager position with a raise of $245 per month."

"I accept the offer." I was thrilled and looked forward to the challenge of being a manager.

Chapter 10: Arrived and Survived

Lockheed Martin was awarded the contract to manage the INL in early 1994. It was exciting, in part, because for the first time the laboratory would be managed by a major corporation. Most everyone had heard of Lockheed Martin.

As part of the transition several management positions were open. The one that caught my attention was the ethics officer. The position was designed to give employees a safe place to report concerns. The Office would investigate allegations of misconduct, provide ethics training, promote ethical conduct, and advise management. I applied for the position and was selected out of the pool of several candidates. This was a senior manager position that reported directly to the president, John Denson.

For the first time in the history of the INL, there was true diversity in the senior management team. During Lockheed Martin's tenure, African Americans held the following positions: executive vice president, VP of engineering, general counsel, EEO/Diversity director, and ethics officer. In the previous forty-five-year history of the INL only one other African American had been in senior leadership. Interestingly, in 1992, Department of Energy Idaho hired David Hamer as their first African American senior manager. Changes were definitely happening at the largest employer in Eastern Idaho.

Being the ethics officer for the laboratory was the pinnacle of my career and something I never could have imagined as the shy, Black kid living in the little shack on the hill.

"Honey, I'm so proud of you," said Monica. Mom and Dad were spellbound as I explained I would be promoting ethical behavior, helping employees, and advising the president of the laboratory. It couldn't get much better than this.

***

On July 15, 1995, my good friend, AJ, president of the local NAACP, reported to the police that while riding his bike with Lori, a white female friend, he was called the N word and threatened by some white people in a van. AJ reported he heard someone say, "Let's kill us a N tonight."

I called AJ the following morning. "Dennis, I thought they were going to run me off the road or perhaps shoot me."

This was one of the scariest stories I'd heard growing up in Idaho Falls. For the rest of the summer I was careful about where I went and who I was with.

As I was reading the *Post Register* on July 31, 1995, an article caught my attention: "Idaho Falls leads Idaho cities in the number of racially motivated incidents and crimes with a total of 15," said Marilyn Schuler of the Idaho Human Rights Commission. I was not surprised, but certainly dismayed that my hometown was the leader in discrimination. It was my hope this information would awaken those committed to fairness and equality.

On December 20, 1995, AJ testified in open court that he feared for his life while on a summer bike ride in July. The accused, Danny DePriest, denied he had threatened AJ. He did testify that he said, "F. you, stupid N." Lori testified she heard a threatening statement from the van. At the end of the trial, DePriest was acquitted on the charge of malicious harassment.

AJ resigned from his position as president of the local NAACP on January 18, 1996. I resigned my position as the Legal Redress

Officer. We both felt it was time to step back for a while. While he didn't say so, I believed AJ was exhausted from the stress of the last few months and disappointed with the outcome of the trial.

Chapter 11: The Unexpected

MONICA DECIDED she no longer wanted to live in Idaho Falls. In October 1997, Lockheed Martin was actively recruiting employees to transfer to other Lockheed Martin facilities. Unfortunately, our marriage was experiencing difficulties at this same time. Monica interviewed for and accepted a job in Sunnyvale, California, only forty-seven miles from her hometown, Berkeley. Darius and Jasmine remained in Idaho Falls with me as I attempted to find a job in Sunnyvale. During the next several months I would fly there with the kids so we could spend time with Monica.

Lockheed Martin hosted its annual 'Employee Recognition Night' on May 8, 1998. It was an event to recognize and honor the 'Outstanding Performers' in their given fields. Mom dressed in a beautiful blue dress she bought especially to accompany me for the occasion.

"That's my son," she would say to anyone within earshot.

"Dennis is commended for the quality of his work in resolving employee concerns in a fair and equitable manner," was the formal citation engraved on the award. President John Denson presented me with the plaque I have always cherished. When I got home, I showed it to Darius and Jasmine.

"Wow, Dad, you must be really important," Darius proclaimed.

I grabbed them both and gave them a big hug. "I love you guys, and that's what's really important."

Sadly, the strain and duress of living in separate households in separate states contributed to Monica and me getting divorced in September 1998. I was blessed to have custody of Darius and Jasmine during the school year. It wasn't easy, but I loved being a dad. We had many great adventures and experiences, along with the challenges of raising two small kids without their mom present. Their grandma, their uncle, aunts, even their older cousins all helped me take care of them.

***

I received my last performance appraisal from Lockheed Martin, John Denson, in August 1999. My rating was 4.8 out of 5.0. I had great memories of the five years, but I also had two experiences I've never forgotten. The first involved an allegation that a manager had authorized funding for something that would be an embarrassment to the laboratory if it was ever disclosed. After completing the investigation, I believed the issue warranted being brought to the attention of John Denson. When the Executive Vice President, Greg Baker, learned of this he called me at home one night.

"Dennis, I understand you're going to speak to Denson," he said.

"Yes, I believe John needs to know."

"I don't think John needs to know. Tell him and you and I are going to bump heads."

I took a deep breath and replied, "My job as ethics officer requires me to make notification."

The phone went dead.

I informed John the next day, but I didn't say anything about the threat.

"Dennis, thanks for letting me know, I'll follow-up." While things were tense with Greg for many weeks, he never followed up on his threat … at least not to my knowledge.

The second event was a whistleblower complaint. In the spring of 1998, an employee, Morris Jim Osborne, reported a dangerous lack of safety inspections at one of the facilities to several Lockheed Martin officials. Two months later the manager requested internal auditor, Doug Benson, to review Osborne's timecard records. This led to a subsequent investigation of timecard fraud by Security.

Based on Security's report, a Review Board was convened. The Board consisted of Osborne's manager; Human Resources; Legal, Dennis Love; Audit, Doug Benson; and me. The Board decided Osborne had committed timecard fraud and the decision was to terminate him.

Osborne filed a whistleblower complaint with the Department of Energy. On September 14 and 15, 1999, a hearing was conducted in Idaho Falls. Dennis Love was the lead attorney representing Lockheed Martin.

The Hearing Officer found Lockheed Martin guilty of retaliation. When I read the final case report I realized the finding was correct and we had failed to protect Osborne's right to report a serious safety issue. Instead, he was fired for doing the right thing.

Later I spoke to him. "Jim, I'm sorry for my role in your termination." Jim accepted my apology and we shook hands.

Chapter 12: Education

DARIUS CAME HOME with a note from Westside Elementary School. It said there had been an incident in the playground and I needed to make an appointment to speak to the principal. I asked Darius what had happened.

"Well, Dad, this red-headed kid was teasing me during recess. He called me a N. We shoved each other and then a teacher came to break it up."

The next day I went to the principal's office. I took a seat opposite her. She explained that Darius and the other kid would need to stay after school for a couple days as punishment for the incident.

"Did you speak to the other student to find out what happened?"

"Yes, I did."

"Did he admit to calling Darius a N?"

"Yes, but I don't see how that's any different than if Darius called him 'carrot top.'"

I couldn't believe the ignorance of a school administrator.

"The N word has been used by whites for hundreds of years to humiliate, denigrate, and oppress African Americans. It is one of the most vile and racist words ever."

She just sat there with a blank look. I don't know if I changed her mind, but she needed to be educated and hear the truth. Afterwards, I made some inquiries and learned she grew up in rural Idaho. Now it made sense. Ironically, the next year a new principal was assigned to Westside School. He was from the San Francisco Bay Area. While visiting the school for an assembly, I shared this experience with him. He expressed surprise and dismay at the reaction of the previous principal. He assured me things would be handled differently in the future.

This experience caused me to wonder how other schools in the area would deal with racist incidents. Was the Idaho native principal an example of what parents of minority children could expect to deal with at school? Did the school districts provide diversity training or resources for the teachers, administrators, and staff? One thing I was sure of; this wasn't the first time, and wouldn't be the last a child would be called N or other racist names at school.

Chapter 13: Another Change

BECHTEL TOOK OVER MANAGEMENT of the INL October 1, 1999. Doug Benson was promoted to Director of Internal Audit. Benson now reported to the President/Laboratory Director, Bernie Meyers. I still managed the Ethics Office, but now I reported to Benson instead of the president. However, as with Lockheed Martin, I continued to have open and free access to the president as needed. Additionally, Bechtel Corporate required an additional level of independence for the ethics officer. As such, I also reported indirectly to the Bechtel Corporate Audit Director. This made it possible for the Ethics Office to investigate and report on matters involving senior management, including the president.

One of the more interesting allegations I received during the early part of Bechtel's management of the INL was reported by an African American. She alleged that the Diversity/Human Resource division had hired an employee who was not qualified for the job. She informed me she had tried bringing this to the attention of management, but no one would listen to her. Now, she was worried that coming to the Ethics Office could result in retaliation.

"Dennis, I'm afraid if they find out I came to you, I might get in trouble."

"No worries; employees have a right to confidentiality and I will honor that."

When I contacted Diversity/Human Resources, I was assured the person hired had a college degree and met all requirements for the job. They also pointed out that she had worked for the company previously as an intern, had an excellent performance history, and was well respected. In spite of this favorable response, I asked to see the person's personnel file. As I reviewed the file, something immediately caught my attention. According to the employee's resume, she completed her bachelor's degree in less than two years. Additionally, her college transcript looked suspect. At this point I requested Security to investigate further.

Security concluded her college transcript had been falsified. Based upon this, and other falsehoods, the decision was made to terminate the employment of this individual. As part of the corrective action, Human Resources was required to implement policies and procedures to prevent this from happening in the future. Throughout the investigation I was able to protect the confidentiality of the reporting employee. However, the working relationship between the Ethics Office and the Diversity/Human Resource department appeared to be damaged by this experience. I was sure Human Resources would have preferred the matter never come to light or be investigated. This incident was particularly embarrassing because it involved Bechtel president Bernie Meyers. His picture, along with the employee's in question, had been on the front cover of a magazine highlighting her success and Bechtel's contribution to her success.

About a year later, my manager, Doug Benson, summoned me to his office. "Dennis, Bechtel Corporate has requested that you conduct an investigation at the Bechtel site in Las Vegas."

Doug went on to explain that an auditor had been accused of conducting personal business on company time and equipment. Under normal circumstances the onsite Internal Audit manager would conduct the investigation. In this case, the accused employee worked for the manager, so it was deemed appropriate to have someone totally independent conduct the investigation. Although I wondered why I had been selected, I was more than happy to spend a few days in Vegas.

After checking into my hotel, I began preparing for the initial interview with the Audit manager. I had met him once before at a Bechtel conference in San Francisco. Monday morning, the receptionist welcomed me and showed me to the office I would use for the interviews. The manager arrived right on time.

"Dennis, good to see you again. I'm looking forward to getting this resolved as soon as possible; it shouldn't take too long."

I was troubled by his remarks. It seemed a bit presumptuous to assume how long the investigation would take. My interview with him lasted over an hour, as I probed not only for facts and figures, but also for possible underlying and contributing issues.

After lunch I was scheduled to interview the accused. I had meticulously prepared my interview questions and was ready to proceed. The door opened. The receptionist came in first, followed by the interviewee.

"Dennis, I would like to introduce you to …"

I looked up and was surprised to see that she was African American. "Welcome, please have a seat." The interview lasted more than two hours. She appeared to be quite forthcoming about her work activities. She provided dates, times, and names of colleagues that, according to her, would prove she was innocent of the accusation.

I spent the next two days reviewing documents and conducting additional interviews. Upon returning to INL, I reviewed my findings with Doug. I did not substantiate the allegation that the person was guilty of conducting personal business on company time. While there were some phone calls and brief correspondence, it was not inconsistent with what other employees were doing. I informed

Doug that there appeared to be some interpersonal issues and possible personal animus between the manager and his employee. I recommended that Human Resources intervene to improve the employee – manager relationship.

I didn't share with Doug my belief that I was selected to go to Vegas because they wanted an African American to investigate an African American. Although I wasn't sent to Vegas to investigate discrimination, I wondered why the Audit manager seemed to treat her differently than her white colleagues.

Chapter 14: Grief and Happiness

MOM DIED FROM PANCREATIC CANCER in May 2002. Her passing was the deepest hurt I had ever experienced. The whole family was with her during the final hours. Together we faced moments when the doctor was hopeful she would recover but then, moments later, declared the end was near. I'll remember forever when Mom asked me to lean down so she could tell me something. She whispered in my ear, "Promise me you'll always keep the family together."

"I promise, Mom," I said, as I kissed her cheek.

Tony Allen, my friend and mentor, sent me a condolence card I've always treasured.

> *Dennis, I was sorry to read in the paper this morning about the death of your mother. I recall with fondness our conversations about family and remembering you with pride and pleasure visiting your mother's family in South Dakota. It was obvious from her obituary the respect and love that is shared by your family and the very special place in that family for your mother. It is apparent the guidance she gave you and developed values in you that you are passing on to your children. The dignity, passion, and compassion that characterize you reflect greatly on her. But it is also a time to celebrate a very successful life and to recall special times, humorous anecdotes and obvious influences your mother had on her family and friends.*
> *Your friends, Tony and Gloria*

The words of my dear friends truly reflected the essence of Mom's life and legacy. The Patterson family would lift each other up with prayer and thanksgiving as we worked through our loss.

Dad died a year later, almost to the day. He had been residing at the Idaho Veterans Home in Pocatello, Idaho. It had been almost seven years since he had been diagnosed with dementia. Placing him in the Veterans Home was the most difficult decision Mom had ever made. During those years, we kids always made sure Mom was able to visit him whenever her heart desired. Dad's funeral service included the traditional military 21-gun salute. The flag draping his coffin was folded and handed to big brother. Mom and Dad left an amazing legacy. My heart was heavy, but filled with a sense of pride and destiny.

***

It was a cold, but sunny day, late November 2003. I was sitting at my desk typing a report when the phone rang. "Dennis Patterson, Ethics Office," I said.

"Hi, Dennis, this is LaVonna."

My heart skipped a beat. LaVonna and I had played golf during the summer and fall, but we were only 'friends.'

She continued, "My work group is having a Christmas party and I was wondering …"

Before she could finish the question, I said, "Yes, I would love to."

She was quick to add, "Of course we will be going as friends."

Well, we had the most amazing time and yes, I was smitten, big time. I proposed to LaVonna less than three months later.

On May 22, 2004, we were married in New Bern, North Carolina. This was her hometown and where her mom, Valderia Brown, still lived. It was a beautiful outdoor ceremony adjacent to the marina on the Neuse River. All my siblings were there, along with nieces and nephews. Darius was my best man. LaVonna's eldest, Valderia Brunson, was the maid of honor. The rest of the wedding party included Valderia's husband, Emanuel; Jasmine; LaVonna's youngest, Patricia; and James Williams, LaVonna's son.

I stood under the white gazebo waiting for my beautiful bride to begin the wedding march. As she came into view, everyone stood. She was absolutely gorgeous in a stunning well-fitted white dress. When she got about halfway down the aisle I made an impulsive, instantaneous decision. I went to get her. I could hear gasps as I grabbed her hand. We walked together to the altar. As we exchanged vows, I looked into her beautiful brown eyes and knew this was my forever love. She smiled that radiant smile as I placed the diamond ring on her finger. We honeymooned in Myrtle Beach, South Carolina. LaVonna had a lifelong love of the ocean and beaches. This would be the first of many beach adventures.

***

Grandpa's Southern BBQ restaurant, the only Black-owned restaurant in southeast Idaho, was the victim of arson on October 2, 2004. My good friends, Lloyd and Loretta Westbrook, were the owners of Grandpa's. The restaurant shared a building with Papa Murphy's Pizza, but only Grandpa's was set afire.

"Dennis, I'm sure it was racism," Lloyd said. Lloyd knew what racism looked like and felt like. He had grown up in Kentucky where hate groups have long called home. Those groups are not unlike the Aryan Nation, a white supremacist organization that called Northern Idaho home in the eighties and nineties.

***

Several months earlier it was announced that Bechtel had lost the contract to manage the laboratory. In late December, I received my final performance appraisal as a Bechtel employee. I was more than pleased when I received the highest rating possible: *Outstanding*.

The following comments were in the write-up:

"Dennis performed several complex and difficult investigations to the highest standard and demonstrated exceptional decision-making skills."

"Dennis' listening skills are outstanding. He has the ability to objectively analyze and resolve complex issues, and has demonstrated the ability to constructively resolve conflict." The appraisal was signed by Doug Benson and Dean Luchsinger, Bechtel Corporate Director of Audit.

In early January, I was summoned to meet with Bechtel's president. He informed me of an accusation that someone had used another's person's work product without proper citation or receiving prior authorization. Because of the sensitive nature of the issue and the need for immediate action, I was asked to review and respond within the week. At week's end I briefed the president on the results. He was appreciative of my quick response, and relieved it was an issue of miscommunication rather than an overt act of plagiarism or theft of intellectual property.

The past five years had been professionally challenging, but also very rewarding. I had investigated a couple of hundred investigations and helped many employees resolve their concerns. I believed I had made a difference in making the laboratory a better place to work. Bechtel's leadership would end at the end of January.

One disappointment during these past five years: not one African American had been in INL senior leadership. For me, it was more than just a matter of equality and fairness. Having representation in the highest levels of management would provide hope and a belief that there was no limit to upward mobility for Blacks at the INL.

Additionally, studies showed that when there is greater diversity in leadership, better decisions are made. Research also demonstrated that diversity reduces the likelihood of group think, which is when like-minded individuals base decisions on conformity rather than facts and reason.

My hope was that Battelle Energy Alliance would value and promote diversity. BEA would assume management of INL on February 1, 2005.

Chapter 15: Race & Racism

THE FIRST WEEK of Battelle Energy Alliance managing the INL was largely uneventful. With Doug Benson still my boss, my job duties remained the same. I reviewed the new organization charts and the new senior management team. I was hopeful there would be more diversity than under Bechtel. Unfortunately, this was not the case. Specifically, there wasn't a single African American in senior leadership. While disappointed, I was hopeful INL had a bright future and I had a bright future. That year would mark my twenty-fifth INL anniversary and my fiftieth birthday.

BEA had been selected to transform INL into the nation's preeminent nuclear research, development, and demonstration laboratory. Excluding the State government, INL was the largest employer in Idaho. According to a recent press release, a guiding BEA principle was 'respect and care for our people.' The question I had was, is this really how BEA would operate the INL or was this just a credo to make employees and the community feel good?

The new laboratory director, president John Grossenbacher, was a retired vice admiral and commander of the U.S. Navy Submarine Forces. After thirty-three years of military service, he was now leading a Department of Energy facility. For me, this didn't bode well for the INL and the work environment. The military, known for its strict command and control leadership, operated nothing like the INL. By federal regulations, DOE facilities were required to have programs for employees to report concerns without going through the traditional management chain. Regulations also provided for anonymous and confidential reporting without fear of retribution. The Ethics Office was established ten years ago and had addressed over a thousand employee concerns, conducted hundreds of investigations, and never once violated confidentiality. It was unclear to me how a military commander would adapt to this very different environment.

I spoke to Doug about my concerns and suggested that I be afforded the opportunity to meet with Grossenbacher to share with him the purpose and objective of the Ethics Office. Doug seemed to understand why I was concerned, but he was quick to add, "Dennis, there is no need for you to meet with him; besides, he's way too busy." I decided to let it go.

On Thursday, February 24, 2005, I was sitting at my desk. It had been a slow day. In fact, there hadn't been any ethics issues reported since BEA took over the contract, just over three weeks before. It was near the end of the day and I was a bit lost in thought. For the past ten years I had two phones on my desk. One was for routine questions, request for guidance, even personal use. The other was the hotline, kind of like the 'bat phone,' used typically for high priority, emergency calls. The loud ring of the hotline startled me.

"Dennis Patterson, Ethics Office."

"I need someone to help me." The voice was a mix of anger, confusion, and desperation. "My name is Loren Mitchell. I'm a construction worker, and I've just been fired. They took my INL badge and escorted me from the job site.

"I need help; no one will tell me why I've been fired and had my badge revoked. When I asked the job supervisor, who escorted me from the premises, he said I already knew why."

Loren explained that on his way home he called BEA Personnel Security (the department responsible for INL badges). The supervisor, Jodi Streier, told him, "It's because of your felony and ongoing problems with the law."

Loren said he explained to her that he had been similarly escorted from the work site eight years ago (1997) because of a felony conviction in 1994. He said he told Jodi his INL badge had been restored in 1998 when he was no longer on probation. According to Loren, none of this seemed to matter. She refused to provide him any further information. Loren said he had received his most recent badge approximately a month ago and had been working with no problems or incidents.

"Dennis, it's not possible for my felony to be the reason for all this. And I haven't had any problems with the law in several years."

Loren added that he even called the company attorney, Dennis Love. Allegedly Love replied, "We don't have to tell you anything. Idaho is a right-to-work state." Loren said he asked if there was an appeal process and was told no.

"Dennis, can you find out why my badge was revoked and why I was fired, and if there is any way to appeal?"

"Yes, I will find out the answers and get back to you."

While I had no knowledge of this particular issue, I was confident this would be resolved soon. I'd make a few phone calls, get the answers, and respond to Loren. In my twenty-five years at INL, I had never known a situation where a person had been terminated without being told why. Everyone had the right to due process.

In most cases, I would independently begin an inquiry to gather information. But in this case, I knew I should inform my boss, Doug, before initiating any action. I deemed this necessary because the issue involved an attorney and two supervisors.

Additionally, Loren was a distant relative (first cousin once removed). Because of this family relationship, those involved might think I couldn't be objective and impartial. I was further concerned that some might see this as just one African American trying to help another. I had experienced this type of bias before.

Benson and I decided to consult with BEA General Counsel, Mark Olsen. Benson placed a speaker phone call to Olsen and we reviewed the facts. It was agreed that it would be appropriate for me to find out why Loren was terminated, badge revoked, escorted from the site, and if there was an appeal process.

We also discussed my family relationship with Loren. I told them that his mother was a cousin of mine, but Loren and I barely knew each other. Benson, Olsen, and I expected this would be a simple procedure review, a few phone calls, and then someone would inform Loren of the results.

When I returned to my office, I decided the first step would be to contact Jodi, the Security Supervisor. I was confident she would share the reason(s) for revoking Loren's access and that due process had been followed. The next morning, I invited her to my office. Jodi and I had known each other for many years. Thus, I began by sharing some life pleasantries and asked how she was doing. The conversation was relaxed and comfortable — until I asked her about Loren.

Jodi explained that the primary reason for revoking his INL badge was his 1994 felony. She said Loren had 'ongoing problems with the law' such as trespassing and burglary. This answer bewildered me because Loren had explained to me that he had been taken off probation in 1998 and had been working during construction seasons at the lab every year since without any problems. It made no sense that he would lie about something that could easily be checked out. I asked Jodi whether these 'problems with the law' were recent. With a quizzical look on her face, she replied, "I don't know."

She reiterated that Loren had a "pattern of problems with the law. Scum bags shouldn't be working here," she added. I inferred that she thought Loren was a scumbag.

"What kind of people do you want working at the Lab?" Jodi asked.

"Those who meet the criteria defined in our procedures," I responded.

Jodi confirmed that Personnel Security had issued Loren an access badge every year since 1998. She emphasized the decision to revoke the access was not just her own. She stated authoritatively that she consulted with and received concurrence from Legal. At the end of the meeting I asked if I could review Loren's personnel security file so that I could validate and verify his supposed ongoing problems with the law. I received an abrupt "no."

Later that same day, Loren called and asked if he could stop by and show me his county court records. We met in a room near Jodi's office. The documents revealed he had a felony conviction in 1994 for working while receiving unemployment benefits and he had been off probation since 1998. There were several misdemeanor violations during 1992 through 1994, including trespassing and battery. However, what caught my attention was that since 1998 the only offenses were fishing with two poles, running a stop sign, and a speeding ticket.

"Looks like you've turned your life around over the past few years," I commented.

"Yeah, I decided it was time to grow up and be a good example and father for my kids. Now I just want to go back to work."

The next day I invited Jodi back to my office to explain what appeared to be a number of unanswered questions. I handed her Loren's court records. After reviewing them, she declared that she still believed he had a pattern of problems with the law. I agreed that from 1992 to 1994 he definitely had a string of legal problems. I asked if I could see Loren's file.

"No," she barked.

I asked, "Is there an appeal process for construction workers?"

Defiantly, she said, "No, there is not."

I ended the interview. Later that afternoon, I briefed Benson on the tone and content of my discussion with Jodi. He seemed surprised by what I told him, but didn't express any particular concern.

Some days later, Loren's local union representative called me.

"Dennis Patterson, Ethics Office," I answered.

"Hey, are you Pat's son?" Pat is the name my father was known by throughout the city. My dad had been a member of Laborers' Local 155 for nearly fifty years.

"Yes," I proudly responded.

"Your dad was a good man, and a hard worker," he informed me. After a brief stroll down memory lane we discussed Loren's situation.

"Dennis, I don't know what you've been told, but BEA does have an appeal process, and it's been used in the past. I don't think Loren is being treated fairly. Right now, there are other union workers on the same job as Loren who have much worse criminal histories." When he said 'other union workers,' I was sure he was talking about white workers. After all, this was Idaho Falls. He said he would fax me a copy of the BEA Appeal Procedure for construction workers.

After hanging up, I leaned back in my chair and closed my eyes. It had been awhile since I had thought about my dad. I had no doubt that if he were alive, he would be most interested in what was happening right now. When he was vice president of Local 155, he fought hard for the rights of its members.

Later that afternoon I received the fax from the union representative. It was titled, "BEA Appeal Process for Construction

Workers." Upon reviewing the procedure, it was clear to me that it applied to Loren's case. If followed properly, the appeal process could help resolve Loren's problem. But my question was, why didn't anyone within BEA tell Loren or me about the procedure?

The next day, I met with Jodi's boss, Lynn Goldman, Security Director.

"Lynn, please convene an appeal hearing as required in the procedure," I formally requested.

Goldman replied dismissively, "This procedure doesn't apply to Loren."

Annoyed and exasperated, I challenged his opinion. "Of course it applies. He's a construction worker!"

Goldman continued to disagree and walked off with a shrug of indifference.

Several days later sanity prevailed and an appeal hearing was convened. I was invited to attend along with Jodi, Dennis Love, Julie Piper, BEA Human Resources Director, and a Labor Relations representative. I had reservations about this meeting, because up until that point, no one seemed to have been honest and forthright.

However, the evidence was overwhelming. Loren had been granted an INL badge for the past eight years and had only very minor problems with the law during that time. The BEA procedure clearly and unambiguously stated: "A person with a felony could work at the laboratory as long as he was no longer on probation." Finally, Loren's work history was void of any performance or behavior problems.

In spite of my reservations, I entered the meeting confident there would be a fair and just outcome. I came prepared with Loren's arrest record, relevant procedures, and a copy of the INL Standards of Conduct and Business Ethics (SOCBE). I expected to attend the entire meeting.

However, after I provided the information, I was told, "Dennis, you can leave now."

I was shocked and bewildered to be asked to leave. It made no sense. I had participated in countless discipline hearings in the past. My initial thought was to defend my right to remain, but instead chose to acquiesce.

Before leaving, I quoted from the SOCBE, reminding everyone of their responsibility to "demonstrate the highest level of honesty and integrity."

I went back to my office expecting to hear good news within the next couple of hours. After waiting most of the day, I contacted the Labor Relations representative, who said, "The appeal was denied." I fell back in my chair and almost tipped over. I couldn't believe what I heard.

"Why was it denied?"

"Well, after you left the meeting someone said Loren had five problems with the law that he didn't report on his security paperwork."

"What are the problems and when did they occur?"

"We were instructed not to tell anyone, but the information is public record."

I considered the possibility that the court records Loren had provided to me previously may have been falsified or otherwise invalid. I left work and went down to the Bonneville County courthouse and reviewed Loren's publicly available arrest records.

Upon entering the building, I went upstairs to the law library, logged onto the computer, and performed the search. The data was an exact match of the information Loren had provided. Not a single 'problem with the law' warranted the actions taken against Loren or justified the decision of the appeal committee. In fact, the evidence strongly suggested that someone in the meeting had either lied or had bad information. I was extremely upset and angry about this apparent miscarriage of justice.

After returning to work, I went to Benson's office and shared the results of the appeal hearing and my research. I was surprised to learn that he already knew the results of the hearing.

"Dennis, you got what you wanted. An appeal hearing was conducted, you presented your evidence; it's over."

"No, it's not over, Doug; we have an obligation to pursue this matter. The evidence does not support the actions and decisions. I'm not going to close the investigation."

Benson's face turned red and his eyes bulged.

"We've done all we are required to do; we followed procedure and held the appeal hearing."

"Doug, it's not about some damn procedure; it's about doing the right thing."

I returned to my office only long enough to turn off my computer. I left for home disappointed, frustrated, and angry.

That night I tossed and turned, wondering what the next day would bring. Would Benson support me on this or would he insist that I let it go? The next morning when I turned on my work computer, I got my answer. I was relieved when I read the email Benson sent to Goldman. He told him the Ethics Office would not be closing the case until we knew what the alleged problems were with the law. I was relieved that for now I had the support of my boss, but I wondered if it would be enough.

CHAPTER 16: Protection and Deception

BASED ON THE FACTS, this was an egregious miscarriage of justice. The biggest challenge was that it involved managers and senior attorneys. It appeared that people were willing to do anything to protect their jobs, reputations, and avoid having to admit to wrongdoing.

One of my first actions was to begin to document my communications with Olsen and Benson. In emails, I expressed my concern that there was the potential for legal liability for BEA. I detailed problems including violations of BEA procedures, abuse of authority, failure to cooperate with my investigation, and possible discrimination. Furthermore, federal laws including the Privacy Act and the Freedom of Information Act may have been violated. I was hopeful that BEA General Counsel, Mark Olsen, would quickly intervene and reduce the risk to the company.

Unfortunately, it didn't happen.

During the next few weeks, I tried to get someone — anyone — to see that Loren had been the victim of a grievous injustice. Sadly, the response was quite the opposite. Now I was targeted and attacked by the very people who had unjustly persecuted Loren.

Benson informed me that Goldman, Streier, Love, and Piper were claiming I was wrong for being involved with this matter because Loren was a relative. I reminded him that I had disclosed my family relationship from the very beginning. I referred to the BEA Employee Handbook wherein the definition of immediate family did not include children of cousins.

Finally, I told Doug, "It's not me who hasn't been impartial; it's them." The most troubling aspect of this was that the only people I had told I was related to Loren were Benson and Olsen. Outside of my disclosure there was no apparent way for others to know Loren and I were distant cousins.

I pointed out that Love and Piper had known each other and worked for Olsen for several years. In addition, Olsen had worked closely with Goldman and Streier as well. "Doug, I believe this is why Olsen hasn't intervened to correct this injustice."

Benson seemed to discount all my concerns. The focus was now on me. I was the trouble maker. No one seemed at all concerned about Loren.

I wondered if things would be different if Loren was a relative of theirs.

I wondered if the accused was someone of importance rather than a Black construction worker.

I wondered if things would be different if I were white or Mormon.

Over the years I had seen unqualified white individuals hired because their spouse was a manager. I had seen a manager hire his Mormon bishop to work for him. I had seen an African American drafter get laid off instead of less qualified white colleagues.

In my opinion this was a classic example of white privilege. According to Francis E. Kendall, author of *Understanding White Privilege,* white privilege is "having greater access to power and resources than people of color (in the same situation) do." Neither Loren nor I had access to power or resources.

A member of BEA's legal staff, Bob Peralta, told me, "John

Grossenbacher will be more concerned about your family relationship with Loren than anything else." For me, this was a thinly veiled attempt to intimidate me and get me to back off my pursuit of justice for Loren.

In spite of all the resistance, I had to pursue this matter because it was the right thing to do and it was my responsibility as INL ethics officer.

A couple of weeks after the appeal hearing, Benson sent this email to me:

Dennis Love indicated there were other factors; he left things out of his application. The implication was the individual falsified his application. That is enough for a site walk-off for me, but I don't recall that ever coming up in discussions with Jodie.

I responded:

Doug, I think Love is just protecting his friends and colleagues. He could care less about whether we are being fair to Loren.

I explained to Doug that I had interviewed an employee of Streier. The employee told me she personally completed the security portion of Loren's application and she used a copy of Loren's arrest record to do so. Therefore, it was impossible for Loren to be guilty of leaving 'things out of his application' or falsifying his application.

Love had also sent emails to Benson wherein he refused to disclose the five alleged problems with the law. Further, Love was adamant in his position that Benson and I had no right to see Loren's personnel security file.

The most confounding part of Love's actions was the fact that he had no authority to make decisions about access to the subject files. Yet he was acting as a roadblock to the very records that could put this matter to rest.

Even more surprising was that Mark Olsen, BEA General Counsel, was unwilling to intervene. Additionally, Benson was the

BEA director of Internal Audit, and as such had full authority and responsibility to demand access to the files.

I was increasingly frustrated about how things were going. Loren's case could be cleared up in a moment's notice if Benson and/or I were allowed to look at the file. If there were problems with the law he had failed to disclose, we could tell him what they were. This would be more than enough reason to revoke Loren's INL badge.

We were now approaching mid-April 2005. As the days and weeks passed, I became more and more worried about how this would turn out. The morning of the 14th, which happened to be my fiftieth birthday, I received an email from Benson. The email was one he received from Love:

While it is true I agreed that if they need access to information in the file in the performance of their duty, they would get it, I also clearly stated that I do not believe they need access to the file in this case because all of the concerns have been addressed. I specifically mentioned that I am aware of cases where the Inspector General wanted access to certain Privacy Act files on individuals as part of their investigation but the court found they did not need them in performing their duty. Please explain why they need access.

Benson responded to me via email at 10:45 a.m.:

Dennis Love considers the issue closed and remains of the opinion that 'nothing' can or should be shared from the file.

"Damn, what a way to begin my fiftieth birthday," I said aloud, hoping no one heard me as they passed by my office.

I shut down my computer and left for home. I needed to be with the love and encouragement of my family and was hoping for a quiet evening with LaVonna and the kids.

When LaVonna got home from work she said, "Let's go out to dinner." I didn't really want to go out, but when the kids yelled "Yay" I couldn't say no. We ended up at Cavanaugh's restaurant. When we entered the room, friends and family jumped out and yelled "Surprise!" I was definitely surprised. I was also glad that Lavonna had invited everyone to celebrate my birthday with us.

Benson and his wife Cindy were among those in attendance. Benson and I had been friends for the past several years. In spite of the work difficulties, it was good to see him. I had also developed a good relationship with Cindy over the years. She had a kind and gentle spirit, with a love for people.

It was a fun evening with lots of laughs and good stories. Those few hours were a great respite from the trials and tribulations I was going through. However, there were moments of pause when I looked at Benson and wondered why he had allowed this matter to drag on so long. Would he eventually do the right thing? Would he have the courage to stand up to Love and BEA managers like Olsen and Goldman?

On April 22, two months after Loren's hotline call, Benson and I were granted access to the file. We scrutinized every page, looking for problems with the law that would prohibit Loren from working at INL. We reviewed to the very last word on the very last page.

We looked at each other — stunned. Benson's jaw dropped and his face went white. I sensed that he felt betrayed by his friends and colleagues.

Loren had no reportable problems with the law since 1997. In fact, there were notes in the file confirming that Loren had been granted access to the INL shortly after getting off probation in 1998 and every year since. There was nothing to support the derogatory information in Dennis Love's email, the revocation of Loren's INL badge, or his subsequent termination.

Benson and I went to Jodi's office. As she looked up her face was flushed and her lip quivered. Benson began, "We completed our review and found nothing to support the contention that Loren had ongoing problems with the law."

She looked away and up at the ceiling.

Benson continued, "How do you explain this?"

"Well, he's either been lucky and hasn't been caught or has learned how to manipulate the system," Jodi said.

Cold chills went through my body. Did I really hear what I thought I heard? For me, this was racism at its worst.

Jodi couldn't accept even the possibility that a Black man had learned from his mistakes.

The silence in the room was deafening.

Benson and I stood up to leave. Jodi said, "Dennis doesn't like me — if he saw me in the parking lot, he'd probably like to run me over."

I expected Benson to respond to the statements about Loren and me. He didn't.

Benson and I walked upstairs to his office.

"Doug, I believe the comments made by Jodi were unprofessional, inappropriate, and discriminatory. For her to say what she said about Loren shows a racial bias. To believe a Black man can't turn his life around; really? And for her to say I want to cause her harm is outrageous."

Benson gave me a blank stare, then changed the topic to the content of Loren's file. He said he would inform Goldman of the results.

"Dennis, I expect Loren's INL badge will be restored in the next few days."

Chapter 17:

Discrimination, Intimidation, and Retaliation

TWO WEEKS PASSED and nothing had happened. Benson said little, except to insist that Loren's case was under review.

After further reflecting on Jodi's statements about Loren and me, I came to believe more strongly that there was racial discrimination. I believed it was a factor in Loren's badge being revoked; managers refusal to cooperate with my investigation; Dennis Love blocking access to the file; and according to Benson, Love's implication that Loren had falsified his application. I also remained puzzled by Mark Olsen's failure to intervene and resolve this matter.

I decided to send an email to Arantza Zabala, BEA Equal Employment Opportunity (EEO) manager and asked to meet with her. I notified Benson via email. He responded promptly, letting me know he was disappointed that I was reporting this matter. He made it clear he was unhappy with me alleging that BEA management was guilty of discrimination.

On May 9, 2005, I met with Zabala. I told her of Jodi's comments and my opinion that discrimination was a factor in actions taken with Loren's case. I expressed my opinion that if Loren had been the 'right' race (white) or the right religion (Mormon), it was likely his INL badge would never have been revoked. And if it had been, the matter would have been resolved in days rather than months.

I also shared my concern that my being African American trying to help another African American may have led my colleagues not to take the matter seriously. I encouraged Zabala to validate and verify that Loren's treatment was consistent with that of other employees.

I was disappointed, but not surprised by Zabala's reaction to my concerns. She barely took notes and her face was stoic throughout our conversation. Zabala and Jodi had worked together for many years and were good friends. Jodi's boss, Lynn Goldman, was also a good friend of Zabala. The same was true about Dennis Love and Julie Piper. All knew each other well and trusted each other.

According to statements from Loren and his union representative, there were other construction workers working at INL with much more serious and recent violations of the law.

I was personally aware of white engineers and administrators who had worse criminal records than Loren. A couple of these employees worked in the BEA Security department. I forwarded this information to Zabala for her to use as part of her investigation.

It had been a month since I filed my discrimination complaint and forty-seven days since Doug had told me, "Dennis, I expect Loren's INL badge will be restored in the next couple of days."

On June 8, because no action had been taken, I met with Cal Ozaki (Lynn Goldman and Jodi Streier's boss). I informed him of the various procedure violations, failure to cooperate with the investigation, potential privacy act violations, and potential discrimination. I provided him a written summary. Ozaki seemed vaguely aware of the issues, but knew little of the details. He agreed to review the matter and take appropriate actions.

Approximately two weeks later, nearly four months after I

received the call on the Ethics Hotline, Loren's INL badge was restored and he was allowed to return to work. When I was notified, I slumped in my chair with a deep sigh of relief. It was hard to believe it was finally over. I had never before experienced what I just went through. People whom I had previously liked, and in some cases trusted, had betrayed their ethical responsibilities, violated Loren's right to due process, and failed to uphold the INL Standards of Conduct.

At times the stress and duress of this experience seemed overwhelming. But I knew this came with the job of being ethics officer. The person who suffered the most was Loren. He had gone months without being able to provide for his family, and suffered the indignity of being banned from working at the largest employer in the state.

The following week, Benson and I were sitting in his office discussing the events of the past few months. "Is BEA going to reimburse Loren for any lost time and wages?" I asked.

"No, we don't have to and we're not going to."

"What about an apology?"

Benson glared at me. Defiant, he responded, "Why would anyone apologize?"

At this moment I felt disgust and contempt for someone I used to call my friend. How could anyone not recognize the most basic of human needs? It was as if Benson was void of empathy. I wondered if his reactions would be different if Loren had been white or Mormon like himself. In my opinion BEA had dehumanized Loren. He had been treated as though he had no value, no worth.

Two months after I filed my discrimination complaint, Zabala sent me an email note stating she found no evidence of discrimination. I was disappointed in the outcome, but not surprised. This was much like what happened so many years ago when attorney Dennis Love and EEO had found no discrimination when Monica had been suspended for twenty days without pay.

Zabala failed to provide any facts or evidence supporting her conclusion that there was no discrimination. To do so, like in Monica's case, she would have had to show that white individuals with arrest records similar to Loren's had also had their INL badges revoked.

The truth is, she could not show one case in the decades-long history of the INL where a white person had been treated the same as Loren. Neither did she provide an explanation for Streier's comment that Loren had manipulated the system or had been lucky and hadn't been caught.

On July 17, I sent Benson an email communicating my intent to meet with Laboratory Director, John Grossenbacher. I told him I wanted to share the results of my investigation and the actions of management and legal with Grossenbacher. As ethics officer, I had always had the responsibility and opportunity to meet with the president when there were matters that posed a risk to the company.

Later that day, General Counsel Mark Olsen called me. Benson had apparently told him I planned to meet with Grossenbacher. I told him that in my opinion the actions taken by security, legal, and others made this one of the most egregious acts of misconduct I'd seen in my tenure as ethics officer. When I shared my intent to meet with Grossenbacher, Olsen responded, "Do you really want to take me on?"

For a split second I couldn't breathe. I had just been threatened by one of the most powerful and influential INL managers — the General Counsel.

After regaining my composure, I asked, "What does 'take me on' mean?"

"I will challenge your credibility with Grossenbacher," he replied.

After taking a deep breath, I said, "I will stand on my credibility and integrity."

After hanging up, I sent an email to Benson describing the conversation. I specifically informed him, "Doug, I believe the statement from Olsen was threatening and intimidating, with the intent of keeping me from speaking to Grossenbacher."

I decided in lieu of meeting with Grossenbacher, I would meet with Juan Alvarez, director of Facilities and Site Services. Jodi Streier, Lynn Goldman, and Cal Ozaki reported to Alvarez. The meeting was held on Thursday, August 11.

When Benson and I walked in the room, I was surprised to see Katherine Moriarty. She was an attorney who reported to Mark Olsen. I presented the facts once again and provided a written report to Alvarez. We discussed the security procedure violations, potential privacy action violations, and the failure of management to cooperate with the investigation.

At the end of the meeting I stated, "In my opinion if Loren had filed a discrimination complaint with the Idaho Human Rights Commission, BEA would have lost."

Alvarez's face turned red as he shoved the report in his folder. "This meeting is over," he declared.

As Benson and I walked backed to our offices he said he was very disappointed in me. I told Benson I felt I had simply reviewed the facts and expressed my opinion.

Ironically, on Sunday I would be leaving to attend three days of investigative training at Battelle Memorial corporate headquarters in Columbus, Ohio. I stopped by my office on Friday to finish some work that needed to be completed before my departure. When I opened the door, I found a sealed envelope had been slipped under my door. I opened the envelope and was stunned to see a letter titled, "Response to Findings of Ethics Investigation."

Alvarez had provided a written response less than twenty-four hours after our meeting. Never before had a written response been provided in such a short time. As I read the letter, I felt like I had made a difference. The first four bulleted items acknowledged a measure of responsibility and accountability on the part of Security management, Alvarez's subordinates. Then came the last bullet. I felt as though I had been shot in the chest.

Alvarez wrote about my comments at the end of the meeting: "Dennis demonstrated a lack of impartiality unacceptable for someone in his position. This bias and lack of impartiality was interpreted by my staff to be offensive and threatening, no doubt contributing to their measured response to his inquiries."

My hands shook and my heart pounded. It only got worse when I realized the letter was not addressed to me and I was not on distribution.

Obviously, I wasn't supposed to see the letter. The letter was addressed to Benson with copies sent to Grossenbacher, Lynn Goldman, Arantza Zabala, Mark Olsen, and the Human Resource Director.

It was clear to me that my reputation and career had just been dealt a severe blow. A senior manager describing the ethics officer as lacking impartiality and quoting his managers as saying I was threatening was damning to my credibility and integrity and hence to my career.

At this moment I realized my efforts to do my job to the best of my ability had resulted in retaliation. I felt betrayed by the company that I believed was going to lead the INL to being a world-class laboratory. The words *valuing and respecting our people* rang hollow in my ears.

I left my office with the letter in my hand. Later that evening, I shared what had happened with LaVonna. We both remembered the conversation in early March when we were worried what might happen if I were to pursue justice for Loren. Here we sat, several months later, and we had our answer. BEA senior management had put a target on my back that could destroy my career.

On Sunday, August 14, 2005, I packed and left the family behind as I headed for Columbus. The most important thing I learned from HR Management Solutions' training is that having an opinion and being willing to speak up, is an expectation of the job.

In fact, the instructor said, "If you aren't ready to express an opinion contrary to management's, then you are in the wrong job." She said when you are behind closed doors, "You need to have the courage to let the fur fly."

As I heard this, I understood that a person could only do this if there was a work culture that encouraged open communications and what was often referred to by Grossenbacher as 'institutional honesty.' I knew I exhibited courage by expressing an opinion contrary to senior management, but now I was in the midst of a struggle that could severely impact my future and that of my family.

During the second day of training, the instructor asked for volunteers to role play an incident involving discrimination. I quickly volunteered. An African American female, Demetrei Mitchell, also volunteered. She did a great job portraying a victim of discrimination — and I think I did a good job of playing the role of the investigator of the complaint.

During a break, I took the opportunity to visit with Demetrei.

"Dennis, I didn't know there are Blacks in Idaho. What's it like?"

"It's not so bad; I've had a pretty good life. Wonderful family, good friends, good job. But we had an incident earlier this year where an African American was terminated without cause. It took me almost four months to get his job back."

"I can't believe this kind of thing is still happening."

She mentioned she was the manager of diversity for Battelle Corporate. As we parted I had no idea that in the not-too-distant future Demetrei and I would be meeting again. Only this time, our roles would be reversed, and it would be all too real.

The following week I learned that Juan Alvarez had been promoted to Deputy Laboratory Director. This meant the person who questioned my integrity was now in an even more powerful and influential position.

Chapter 18: We Find Ourselves Not Guilty

During September I sent Benson several emails expressing concerns about what had happened to Loren and what I believed was retaliation against me. On September 8, 2005, I sent Benson an email informing him I had scheduled a meeting with Grossenbacher to be held in October.

Five days later Benson informed me that Battelle Corporate had decided to send a team of investigators out to Idaho Falls to investigate my concerns. My meeting with Grossenbacher was canceled. I should have been surprised, but I wasn't. It was clear that BEA would go to any lengths to make sure I didn't speak to Grossenbacher. And it was my belief that Grossenbacher had already been briefed by Alvarez, Benson, and Olsen. Of course, he likely wasn't being told the truth.

In late October, I received the call. Two investigators from Corporate wanted to interview me on November 2. At last, someone from outside BEA was going to investigate. I was hopeful that justice would finally prevail and that appropriate corrective actions would be taken.

However, in reality, it was next to impossible for a corporation to find itself guilty of misconduct, especially at the highest levels of management. A corporation is incentivized to protect itself, regardless of the impact to the employee.

I called LaVonna and told her about the upcoming interview. She expressed optimism that once the facts were known, I would be rewarded for doing the right thing and my career would be restored.

"LaVonna, I think that is too much to hope for. Let's expect the worse, but hope for the best."

The morning of November 2, my palms were sweating as I waited outside the office where the interviews were being conducted. I said a prayer and reviewed my notes.

The lead investigator, a senior corporate attorney, opened the door, greeted me, and offered me a seat at a round table. I stood frozen for a moment. Sitting at the table was Demetrei Mitchell.

"Good to see you again, Demetrei. Looks like this time we aren't role playing."

"Yes, I've been asked to participate in the investigation of your concerns."

It had been three long months since our first meeting and much had happened.

The interview lasted about four hours. It was like reliving a nightmare. I explained in great detail the events since the initial hotline call in February. I was surprised at the lack of intense questioning and probing follow-up. Although Demetrei and I had attended the same investigative training it appeared to me something was missing.

At the conclusion of the interview, I handed Demetrei a summary of my concerns and allegations. They informed me that over the next several days they would be interviewing security personnel as well as Benson, Olsen, and Alvarez. During the interview I had given them additional names of employees they needed to interview.

Thanksgiving and Christmas came and went without word from anyone about the progress of the corporate investigation. I could feel the stress and burden of waiting for a decision that would likely define my future with INL. After returning from the Christmas holidays, I hoped to hear at least a status report, but nothing. Benson largely avoided me and spoke only when absolutely necessary. I was sure he knew the report could be damaging to his future as director of Internal Audit and Ethics.

In early February I learned the corporate report had been issued to BEA senior leadership. I assumed this included John Grossenbacher. On February 10, I was summoned to meet with BEA senior manager, Art Clark, to review the results of the Battelle corporate investigation.

Clark sat at the table with a copy of the report in his hands. He stated that the report did not find any unethical actions, including intimidation or retaliation, on the part of senior management. He further noted they found no evidence of discrimination. This information was provided rather cryptically, with no elaboration or clarification. Even though I was aching inside and on the verge of throwing up, I held it together. I sat stoically and said nothing.

Clark continued, "Dennis your actions were admirable. You were willing to fight for someone whom no one else seemed to care about." He added, "Benson should never have taken no for an answer when he asked to look at the security file." He stated that Benson could never be successful in a line management role because he wasn't strong enough to take the required actions.

"Dennis, had you come to me early on the matter would have been addressed much sooner. Olsen and Benson didn't do a good job protecting the integrity of the Ethics Office."

Clark noted his opinion that, "Olsen believes that once he makes a decision that is that." He added, "Dennis, the corporate investigation concluded the Ethics Office is in good shape and things there are going well."

At the end of the meeting I said, "Art, something has to be

done about the Alvarez letter because it has damaged my reputation and career."

"I will do my best, but I'll need to find a way for Juan to save face."

I was heartened by Clark's affirmative comments and his intention to address the Alvarez letter. But I was disappointed that none of the intimidating and threatening actions of BEA senior management had been acknowledged. I was outraged they found no evidence of discrimination. Demetrei herself had told me in August that she couldn't believe what BEA had done to an African American. Nonetheless, this was the best I had felt about my career in the past year. For the first time in a long time, I had hope that things were going to work out.

Chapter 19: It Only Gets Worse

ON FRIDAY, FEBRUARY 17, 2006, I went to work expecting to have a great day. During this time, BEA management was conducting annual performance reviews. In spite of the controversies, I was hopeful I would be recognized and rewarded for overturning the injustice perpetrated toward Loren, protecting the interests of BEA, and for my commitment to the INL Standards of Conduct & Business Ethics.

Benson came into my office and sat down at the table opposite my desk. "Dennis, we need to discuss your performance for 2005." As he spoke, he handed me the written appraisal, "Read this and then we'll talk about it."

My stomach tightened, and I could feel my blood pressure rising. Even before reading it, I knew it wasn't going to be good. The words seem to blur on the page as I read each section. When I got to the end, I saw the final overall rating. For the past seven years I had received the highest rating possible: outstanding. The next level down would have been 'excellent.' I didn't get either of those ratings. My rating now was 'good.'

In my opinion, this was the definition of retaliation. DOE regulation 442.1B, "encourages the free and open expression of employee concerns and provides, DOE contractor employees with an independent avenue to raise any concern related to, but not limited to the environment, safety, health, security, quality and management as well as harassment, intimidation, retaliation and discrimination."

I had reported several issues covered by the order, and the result was harassment, intimidation, discrimination, and finally retaliation as evidenced by the low performance appraisal.

"Doug, you know what this looks like?" I knew he did, because he and I were on the losing side of the Morris Osborne whistleblower complaint in the late nineties.

His pale face turned red, his fists clenched, and he squirmed in his chair.

"Doug, Art Clark briefed me on the results from the corporate investigation. It was very favorable in regards to my decisions and actions. This rating does not reflect that. Also, Clark said he would be taking action to address the Alvarez letter."

Benson seemed surprised, but said he would speak to Clark and reconsider the performance appraisal rating.

One week later, Benson knocked on my door, entered, and sat down. He held a piece of paper in his hand. With detached coldness and arrogance, he said, "Dennis your job title has been changed from manager to specialist." He tried to justify the action by noting that I didn't have anyone reporting to me. He added, "By the way, your current salary won't be impacted but the upper salary limit is now two thousand dollars a month lower."

I was taken aback by this blatant and callous act of retaliation. I knew several managers who had no one reporting to them, but they still retained the title of manager. Of course, there were two big differences. First, none of them had reported allegations of misconduct.

And second, all of them were white.

"Dennis, I spoke to Art Clark like I said I would. Art denied making any statement about addressing the Alvarez letter." I wasn't particularly surprised. Clark didn't have the authority to take action, even if he wanted to. There was no way for Alvarez to 'save face.'

At this point I had exhausted all avenues within BEA to resolve my concerns. The only person with more authority than Clark and Alvarez was Grossenbacher. and that door had already been slammed shut.

Chapter 20: Blowing the Whistle

IN EARLY MARCH 2006 I attended the Spring Conference of the Employee Concerns Program Forum in Philadelphia. I always looked forward to the conferences. It was great getting to know folks in similar jobs dealing with similar challenges. It also was an opportunity to meet and interface with DOE Employee Concerns professionals — people who were committed to fairness, justice, and doing the right thing. We always set aside time to share lessons learned and improve our understanding of DOE requirements, regulations, and systems designed to protect workers' rights to report concerns without fear of retaliation.

On the third day of the conference, a special training was offered by Ms. Billie Garde. Billie was an attorney who provided investigation and whistleblower training to corporations and organizations throughout the country.

I was among the first attendees to sign up. Given what I had endured over the past several months, I wanted to learn as much as possible.

Billie, a middle-aged white female, began the training session by sharing her personal story as a former whistleblower. She described a very painful time in her life when she worked for the Census Bureau in Oklahoma. Part of her job was to hire people consistent with the ethnic composition of the region. Over the years, Native Americans had been significantly undercounted. Billie explained that it was important that they, along with other ethnicities, had proper Census Bureau representation. She was professionally and personally committed to hiring more minorities.

Billie said her district manager was more concerned about his own political agenda. He directed Billie to hire only those people who would be of benefit to him, i.e., those who would owe him favors. He went so far as to instruct her to change Civil Service test scores to ensure the right people were hired. He also made sexual overtures to her and told her that the young women she hired had to sleep with local political leaders.

"Class, I refused to follow the instructions from my boss. Not only that, I reported him to the Oklahoma Congressional office and to the Census Bureau's regional director. Not surprisingly, when my boss learned I had reported him, he systematically attempted to intimidate me."

"He called me into his office, threatened me, and told me to keep my mouth shut. He threatened to interfere with the custody arrangements with my children. Later he spread rumors about my sex life and questioned my fitness as a mother. After other females in the office also complained about his sexual exploitation, he fired me."

Billie chose to relocate to the East Coast. Soon after arriving she received a call from an Oklahoma newspaper reporter who was writing a story about the Census Bureau scandal. With some trepidation, she agreed to tell what she knew.

After the story appeared, her boss waged a vicious campaign against her by spreading rumors such as being an unfit mother. He attempted to destroy her credibility and reputation in the community. Unfortunately for her boss, these actions only made her more determined to keep fighting. Along with others, she testified against her ex-boss before a grand jury.

Facing substantial prison time, her former boss pleaded guilty to Conspiracy to Defraud the United States.

Throughout this horrific ordeal, Billie had the strength, courage, determination, and conviction to pursue justice to the end. At the age of thirty, she enrolled in law school and became the director of the Citizens Clinic for Accountable Government. Several years later she opened her own law practice. Since then, she has been assisting whistleblowers, especially those in the nuclear industry.

During the presentation, Billie described the profile of someone who would make the ideal whistleblower. "The person would need to have an excellent performance history, be well respected in the community, and be a person of great integrity and character. And most importantly, have the courage and strength to endure the long and painful journey."

After the training I told Billie how much I admired and respected her. She thanked me and presented me with a Certificate of Training: *Methods to Detect, Prevent, and Investigate Retaliation in the Workplace* signed by Billie Pirner Garde.

As I stared out the window on my flight home, I realized that everything happening in my life had a purpose. God has a purpose for everything and every person. Billie spoke directly to my situation, my character, and my heart. I was on my way home with a sense of peace and purpose. Nothing could deter me now. I knew what I had to do.

Over the next few days, I reflected on the events of the last year. Specifically, my performance appraisal, job title, and merit increase. My training and experience told me the most common method of retaliation was related to performance appraisals and money. I also remained deeply concerned about discrimination and its impact on my career and the Loren case.

What, if any, action was I going to take? Basically, the choices were to do nothing, file a discrimination complaint with the Idaho Human Rights Commission (IHRC), or file a whistleblower complaint with the Department of Energy. I decided to file an IHRC discrimination complaint.

My prior success filing with the IHRC was a factor, but this was also an opportunity to highlight the need for greater diversity at the Laboratory. There had not been an African American senior manager at the lab, including DOE, since 1999. In late March, I prepared my discrimination complaint and faxed it from my office to the IHRC.

Several weeks later, the IHRC sent me BEA's rebuttal to my complaint. It was several pages long with the typical legal jargon I'd come to expect. BEA stated that in no way was race a factor or consideration in any of the actions with Loren or me. I carefully analyzed BEA's response. In doing so, I recognized that my complaint had a significant area of weakness. The most obvious and blatant discrimination actions were the ones BEA had taken against Loren. For this complaint to be successful the IHRC would need to involve Loren. Life had been difficult enough for him already.

I sent an email to the IHRC requesting that they dismiss my discrimination complaint.

I decided to file a government Code of Federal Regulation 708 whistleblower complaint with the U.S. Department of Energy Office of Hearings and Appeals in Washington D.C. I knew that, not unlike Billie Garde, my career and possibly life could suffer severely. There was the distinct likelihood I would be subject to more intimidation, harassment, and possibly termination.

On June 1, 2006, I sent the 708 complaint to Ms. Jan Ogilvie, DOE Idaho Program Manager for Employee Concerns. I had gotten to know Jan pretty well over the past several months. We had developed a good working relationship. She was responsible for oversight of the functions and duties of my office. We both attended the March ECP meeting in Philadelphia, where we received training on investigations, employee rights to file complaints, and whistleblower protections.

I stopped by her office to confirm receipt of the complaint. Jan informed me that my complaint would be reviewed by Beth Sellers, Manager of DOE Idaho, and then sent to John Grossenbacher. While I liked Jan, she had no experience in the field of ethics or employee concerns prior to assuming her position a few months previously. Now she was handling, in my opinion, one of the highest risk, high profile whistleblower cases in INL history: one filed by INL's first African American ethics officer. A complaint alleging the highest levels of INL management of egregious misconduct.

Not unexpectedly, on July 17, 2006, DOE–ID summarily dismissed my whistleblower complaint. To my knowledge, the decision was made without conducting an investigation. I appealed the decision with DOE Office of Hearings and Appeals (OHA) on July 31, 2006. On August 21, 2006, DOE OHA granted my appeal. Once again, I had reason to be hopeful.

That evening I shared the good news with LaVonna. It had been a year and a half since the hotline call that led us down this path. Sadly, I knew from experience the rest of the journey would be much longer and likely more painful. Nonetheless, as long as I had my faith, family, and friends, I knew things would be okay.

Chapter 21: Persecution of a Good Man

A MONTH EARLIER, on May 1, a BEA manager, Kathryn McCarthy, stopped by my office. She came with the hope that my office could be of assistance to an employee. His name was Eric Greenwade. He had spoken to her about unfair and unjust treatment by his manager. She expressed her opinion that there was merit to his complaint, but there was nothing she could do. Eric had performed work for her in the past and thus she knew he was an excellent performer. In fact, she had recently requested his services, but his current manager refused. She told me Eric was afraid his manager would retaliate if he reported the issue to Ethics. I explained I couldn't take any action unless Eric came forward.

It was exceedingly rare for a manager to come to the Ethics Office on behalf of an employee. In fact, this was only the second or third time ever. In this case it wasn't particularly surprising because McCarthy was well known for being fair and ethical with her employees.

A few days later, Eric showed up in my office. His voice quivered. He shifted nervously in his chair. Eric told me about a disagreement with a manager at the end of the previous year. The result of that disagreement, Eric alleged, was a poor performance appraisal and a disciplinary action.

"Dennis, I'm afraid my manager will retaliate against me, maybe even fire me, if you investigate."

"Eric, BEA has a policy against retaliation, but of course there's no guarantee it won't happen."

Eric's face went white, but with a sense of determination he said, "Do it; if it doesn't help me, maybe it will help someone else."

Over the next few weeks, I conducted an extensive investigation. I interviewed Eric's immediate manager, Patrick O'Leary, and the next level manager. I also reviewed Eric's performance appraisal for the prior year. To my surprise, he had received the highest possible rating: Outstanding.

In addition, the appraisal contained a hand written note from the previous Laboratory Director: "Thank you for your significant contributions to the success of the lab."

The record showed that Eric had previously been a 'Laboratory Fellow.' A Fellow was the highest professional designation at INL. This designation meant that Eric was nationally and internationally recognized in his area of scientific study. I reviewed written input from several managers, internal and external to the INL. The feedback was overwhelmingly positive. Eric was well known for his contributions to High Performance Computing. Yet the appraisal Eric had just received rated him 'does not meet expectations,' which placed him at the very bottom of the laboratory.

Only one other INL employee had received this rating and this person had since been terminated. I had never seen a situation where an employee had gone from the best of the best to the worst of the worst in a matter of months.

The other issue Eric reported was the discipline letter. The letter was largely based on the same information in the performance appraisal, with one exception. It quoted another manager as being "disappointed with Eric's performance." When I interviewed that manager, she stated she was more than pleased with his performance and in fact would like him to work for her again. As such, it appeared the information in the appraisal was false or at least misleading.

Eric stopped by my office to check on the status of the investigation. His face was pale and he had lost weight. "Dennis, I can't sleep, don't have an appetite, and I have trouble concentrating at home and at work. And my wife is experiencing the same."

I tried to encourage him and apologized for the investigation taking so long. "Eric, I'm also going through a very stressful time right now. So, believe me when I say I can understand. What has helped me is my faith, family, and friends."

It was another couple of weeks before I saw Eric again. When he arrived, I met him at the door. I could see he looked better. I sensed a level of peace as he began to speak.

"Dennis, I've been doing better since we last spoke. Partly, it's because of what you told me last time. Do you remember what you told me?"

Sheepishly I responded, "Sorry, but I don't."

"You told me about the importance of faith, family, and friends."

We gave each other a hug and wished each other well. I told Eric I would keep him updated.

I sat at my desk and pondered my own situation. My stress level was beginning to worry me. I reflected upon a time a few years earlier. I had just met with an employee who had reported an allegation of unfair treatment. After the person left, my chest started feeling heavy and I felt light headed. I went to the first floor and checked in with the company doctor. I ended up being carted off to the hospital in an ambulance. Fortunately, I didn't have a heart attack, but I was put on blood pressure medication with instruction to watch my stress level. The doctor reminded me of the life-threatening outcomes from the effects of long term, high level stress. This was probably the most stressful time in my life and I wasn't sure when it was going to end.

I completed the investigation of Eric's complaint at the end of June. The evidence overwhelmingly supported his allegation that his performance appraisal and disciplinary action were unfair. On July 10, 2006, I issued the investigative report to the director, Brian Sack. The report substantiated Eric's complaint. I recommended that management reassess the performance appraisal, the disciplinary action, and take appropriate action. I reminded Eric's management of employees' right to report concerns without fear of retaliation.

Within a few days of the issuance of the report, I was contacted by Eric. He said he believed he was being retaliated against for reporting his concerns and for the report I sent to management.

"They revised my appraisal alright; now it's worse than before I came to you. The discipline letter was revised also, but now it has more negative comments. My career is destroyed."

My heart sank; my efforts had only made matters worse. Eric tried to fight back the tears.

"Dennis, my wife and I have decided to leave Idaho Falls. My wife and kids love Idaho Falls, we don't want to leave, but I'm left with no choice." He had opportunities at two DOE national labs that he was seriously considering.

"Would you like to file a retaliation complaint?" I asked.

"Management would only make my life even more miserable."

"I'm so sorry. Eric, you have every reason to be proud of your contributions to the laboratory. The input from those I talked to in my investigation spoke highly of you. People respect and admire you. Unfortunately, your current management failed to honor its obligation to fair and ethical behavior."

"Dennis, I will always be thankful for your efforts."

What a gracious and generous response. While Eric was forgiving, it would be a long time before I could forgive myself for making things worse for a good man.

***

To my delight, I learned much later that Eric had gone on to great success at another national laboratory and at Microsoft. And Kathryn McCarthy went on to be director at another national laboratory. It is a powerful testimony when good things happen to good people.

Chapter 22: African American Alliance

IN 2006 A GOOD FRIEND, Dave Snell, talked to me about some of the challenges being African American and living in Idaho. We discussed lack of diversity at INL, difficulty of African Americans getting hired, lack of African American hair products in Idaho Falls, lack of cultural events, and the absence of African American influence in our community.

Dave and I met at Pastor Patterson's (my big brother) home to discuss further. We brainstormed how we could contribute to improving our community, including INL. As we sat at the kitchen table, I imagined what it must have been like in the 50s and 60s as folks met in churches and pastors' homes during the Civil Rights era.

The following month, we convened a breakfast meeting at a local restaurant. Approximately twenty African Americans attended. There was passionate discussion about a multitude of issues and how we might address them.

Issues included limited ethnic cultural events, lack of ethnic products and services, diversity, racial intolerance, employment, education, and others. A specific concern was the apparent lack of commitment to diversity at the laboratory, including DOE Idaho.

We met weekly to formulate our goals, strategies, and mission statement. Coming up with a mission statement that everyone could support turned out to be an arduous and sometimes painful process.

Finally, we agreed upon the following: "We are committed to initiating dialogue and providing resources that contribute to the educational, cultural, and economic development of our community. And to promote understanding among all races."

We also struggled with coming up with a name for our organization. The consensus was that the organization would be open to everyone and would address a wide range of diversity issues. However, we also wanted a name that would recognize the presence and contribution of African Americans. This was important, in part, because Blacks make up less than 1 percent of the Idaho population. After healthy debate, we agreed on the name "Idaho Falls African American Alliance (AAA)."

We decided that one of our first efforts to make a difference in our community would be to hold an annual banquet in honor of Dr. Martin Luther King, Jr. We would invite keynote speakers from across the country. They would be prominent and influential African Americans who could enlighten, educate, and inspire our community. Further, we would use proceeds from the banquet to award scholarships to African American graduating high school seniors. And finally, we would make annual contributions to charitable organizations and needy individuals.

We scheduled a meeting to elect officers. As the time approached, I spoke with LaVonna.

"Sweetheart, I believe now is the time for me to step up. I would like to put forth my name for president."

"Of course, I think you are the right person for the job. This is your passion."

At the end of the meeting, we walked out together arm in arm, I as the president of the African American Alliance and LaVonna as my biggest supporter.

I felt humbled and honored to have the opportunity to lead an organization that was committed to improving our community. I was also honored to have an amazing leadership team that included LaDonna Foster, Vice President; Roberta Jordan, Secretary; and Marilyn Standfield, Treasurer.

I had no idea a member of our team would later file a discrimination complaint herself.

Chapter 23: A Different Kind of Discrimination

ONE WARM, SUNNY SUMMER DAY in July, I returned to my office after visiting a friend in another building. I was having a very routine day when my phone rang. The caller identified himself and said he wanted to report a concern. He told me that he and some other employees had posted flyers on company bulletin boards and that some unknown person had removed them. He said he believed his religious freedom was being compromised.

I asked him why this was a religious matter. He said that several employees had decided to hold a prayer breakfast at a local park. The flyer was posted to let all interested employees know about the breakfast.

The purpose was to pray for the welfare of the laboratory and employees. The flyer contained the words *prayer breakfast* and provided the date, time, and location. He wondered if I could follow up to find out why the flyers were removed and see if they could be reposted. I agreed to do so.

I discovered that the Diversity Office and Legal Office had decided it was inappropriate to allow employees to post information on bulletin boards that included a reference to prayer. Their position was that allowing such flyers would give the impression the company supported the event. They further reasoned it would make non-Christians feel uncomfortable.

I was copied on several emails sent by a friend, John Howze. John worked in the Communication and Public Affairs division. The emails were sent to Legal and Diversity. John cited several references that, in his opinion, contradicted the company's position and, in fact, suggested it might be illegal for the company to prohibit the posting of the subject flyers. I then sent emails to Diversity and Legal wherein I stated my support of John's position.

After the exchange of several emails between John, Diversity, Legal, and me, it became clear that sending emails was not an effective approach to resolving this issue. John and I sent emails requesting the opportunity to meet with Legal and Diversity face to face. We wanted to have open and direct communications and hopefully come to a resolution acceptable to both sides of this issue.

To our surprise, General Counsel, Mark Olsen, and the manager of Diversity, Arantza Zabala, refused to sit down and talk to us. They said they would accept emails from us but were adamant that no face-to-face discussions would occur. In response to this arrogant attitude, I sent an email to Benson requesting that he intervene and help facilitate the opportunity to have dialogue about this matter. He refused. I suspected Olsen and Benson's refusal had little to do with this matter and everything to do with the fact that I was the person trying to help an employee. As with the Mitchell matter, I was trying to do my job, and they were refusing to cooperate.

A few days later, John informed me that Legal had contacted his manager and told him John was causing problems and it needed to stop. John and I believed this was another example of Legal trying to intimidate someone in response to raising a concern. Afraid of being fired, John decided to take no further action. I fully agreed with John's decision. I had already been the victim of Olsen's wrath.

In the process of pursuing the flyer issue, I decided it would be appropriate to revisit a previous controversial subject. In early 2005,

The *Post Register* ran a front-page story about an INL policy prohibiting employees from holding Bible studies on laboratory premises. Zabala was quoted as strongly defending the policy and was adamant that no change was forthcoming.

From a fairness perspective, and as a Christian, I disagreed with the policy and hence decided to conduct my own research on the matter. I contacted colleagues at other DOE national laboratories and discovered that these laboratories allowed Bible studies as long as they were held during lunch or before or after work.

I then sent emails supporting a change in policy to Legal and Diversity. After several weeks of heated debate, Legal and Diversity agreed to change company policy and allow employees to hold Bible studies consistent with other laboratories. Again, an issue that should have taken a few days took several weeks.

The company issued an iNote (an email message that is the standard vehicle for BEA to communicate with the work force) to all employees. The iNote contained good news and bad news. The good news was that holding Bible studies on the premises was now acceptable. The policy also allowed for discussion of religion among employees as long as both parties were comfortable. An employee could actually share his/her faith with others without fear of getting in trouble. The bad news was that posting anything religious (including reference to prayer) was still prohibited.

Because of the last ruling, the prayer breakfast flyers were never allowed to be posted. In spite of this, the event was held as scheduled. Those of us in attendance prayed for each other, our community, and the INL. Over the next year, the prayer breakfast continued as a small, tightly knit weekly prayer meeting held at the homes of INL employees. Prayers regularly went forth for the INL and its employees. I was blessed by meeting fellow Christians and building prayer partners who cared about the INL and about me.

Chapter 24: Nightmare

JUNE 2006 was a month to remember. I became president of AAA and I filed a DOE whistleblower complaint. Both events would turn out to be defining moments in my life.

I never thought I would become a whistleblower. During the past twelve years as ethics officer, I had helped the company defend itself against whistleblowers. I knew the journey of a whistleblower was long, painful, and expensive. I knew that in most cases, if not all, it was a death knell to the whistleblower's career.

My personal burden had become heavy and the stress sometimes unbearable. Already I had received an unfair performance appraisal, been demoted, and my reputation damaged by the Alvarez letter. Now, I was worried BEA would take even more drastic actions based on the fact that I filed the complaint with DOE. LaVonna's biggest worry was my health. As a psychologist she knew the emotional, mental, and physical damage that could result from long-term high stress.

On Thursday, July 13, 2006, my day began as usual. It was a beautiful sunny morning. I poured myself a steaming cup of coffee and went out on the deck for some quiet time before leaving for work. As I sat there, Ziggy, our black playful cocker spaniel, jumped in my lap. I stroked her soft coat as she licked my face. I was thankful to have a beautiful home and a loving family. Before leaving for work, I gave LaVonna a kiss.

She said, "Have a great day."

I was at work sitting at my computer when the phone rang.

"My name is Torrance; I'm an investigator with BEA Security. I need to meet with you in a half hour, in my office," the deep voice boomed with authority.

My heart pounded and I could hardly breathe as I realized I was being investigated.

"Why do you need to meet with me?"

"I can't tell you why."

"Look, I'm a trained investigator and I know you can tell me if you want to."

"Okay, you are under investigation for misuse of government equipment."

My gut wrenched and my head felt like it was going to explode. Composing myself, I responded, "I'll be down to your office in thirty minutes, maybe sooner."

My trembling hand dropped the receiver back in its cradle. This was surreal. It felt like a horrible nightmare. Instinctively, I knew this was harassment and retaliation. BEA had found out about my whistleblower complaint just ten days before and now I was being investigated for the first time in my twenty-six-year career.

For several minutes I tried to calm myself. I prayed, "God please protect me, please help me prepare for what is coming, give me the strength and courage to persevere, allow me to face this with dignity and humility."

I knew I had not misused government equipment or time, but I also knew that being innocent doesn't mean you won't be found guilty — especially if you are Black.

Being innocent didn't keep Loren from losing his job.

Being innocent didn't keep Monica from being suspended for

twenty days.

Yes, I was innocent, but I needed to do everything I could to protect myself and my family.

I arrived at Torrance's office twenty-five minutes after his call. He welcomed me into his office and reiterated that he was asked to investigate me for misuse of government time and equipment.

"Dennis, it will be best if you tell the truth." He then turned on a recording device and placed it on the table.

"Dennis, have you ever misused government equipment?"

"Absolutely not, I want to know who has accused me of this."

"Management requested that I investigate you, but that's all I can tell you."

"Have you ever received or sent personal emails from your work computer?"

"Of course I have, as allowed by company policy."

"Give me some examples."

"I sometimes communicate with family and I have communicated with members of the African American Alliance. Company policy allows me to send the emails related to the African American Alliance for two reasons. First, it only took a few minutes of time and second, the AAA mission supports the diversity initiative of the company."

"Anything else?"

"Yes, I sent emails to the Idaho Human Rights Commission requesting the dismissal of my discrimination complaint and to DOE regarding my whistleblower complaint."

When I provided this information, his eyes opened wide, he sat up in his chair and leaned toward me, his arm muscles tensed. His body movements reminded me of an animal that had his prey cornered with no way to escape.

Of course, things aren't always what they seem.

"Torrance, you may not know this, but company policy allows me to use time and equipment to file both my discrimination complaint and the whistleblower complaint."

Torrance's face went blank and he leaned back in his chair. It was like the air suddenly escaping from a balloon. After regaining his composure, he targeted my actions related to my whistleblower complaint.

"Did you prepare the whistleblower complaint on your work computer and if so, how much time did you spend?" he asked.

"Yes, I charged approximately four hours of time. Torrance, you may not know it but doing so was completely within company policy and DOE regulations."

Again, Torrance slumped back in his chair. This interview hadn't gone as he had planned, or had been told it would go. He closed his notebook and turned off the recording device.

"Dennis, when I complete my investigation, I'll provide a report to management and they will determine if there will be any disciplinary action. Thank you for being cooperative; you know it's not uncommon for the interviewee to be combative. I appreciate the fact that you have been forthright and cooperated fully."

"Torrance, you're just doing your job." We shook hands as I left his office.

Returning to my office, I needed the soft comforting voice of LaVonna. I took a couple of deep breaths. I knew I was innocent but struggled with the idea of calling and telling her I was under investigation. Finally, I placed the call.

She answered, "Hi, Babe, you having a good day?"

"No, sweetheart. I don't even know how to say this; I'm being investigated by Security for misconduct. This could lead to my termination."

"I love you, and I know you haven't done anything wrong. God will see us through this. I'll see you when you get home."

Misuse of government equipment was a termination offense. I needed to respond immediately. I reviewed all the emails I had sent and received since January. Out of the 950 or so emails, I counted 40 that were not work-related. I also calculated an estimate of the amount of time I had spent writing and/or reading the emails related to the discrimination complaint and my whistleblower complaint.

At the end of the day, I sent an email to Torrance and his boss, Tom Middleton. Tom was the director of Security and also happened to be my next-door neighbor. His kids were friends with Darius and Jasmine. In my email I documented that my actions were clearly within company policy and DOE regulations. I forwarded the same emails to Mark Olsen. It was imperative that I get this information into the appropriate hands before I got fired. I knew from my experience with Loren, once BEA made a bad decision it was next to impossible to turn things around. Especially if you didn't have someone fighting for you. I had no one.

I needed a definitive answer as to whether writing a whistleblower complaint on INL equipment was timecard fraud or any other violation. I sent an email to BEA Prime Contract Manager, Lisa Sehlke. She had authority and responsibility for this issue.

On July 24, 2006, she responded via email. "Inasmuch as the requirements for filing a complaint under the Whistleblower Act are included in the BEA contract and as long as the time charged for completing the form is considered reasonable, the time an employee uses to write his/her complaint is an allowable cost under the contract. Use of contractor phone and email on company time to complete the complaint in accordance with the contract requirements is also an allowable cost."

I immediately forwarded this to Benson and Olsen. I thought this would be the end of it.

The next day Olsen sent me an email challenging Sehlke. He said it was against company policy for me to write my whistleblower complaint on my work computer. To me, this was simply another extreme example of arrogance and a refusal to admit he was wrong. I responded to his email with references to DOE regulations and informed him that never before had the INL taken such a clearly indefensible position.

I then received an email from DOE–Idaho attorney Eva Auman, a colleague of Olsen's and whose opinion he had already solicited. In the email, she wrote, "In my personal opinion, an employee who files a complaint against his or her employer (in any industry) should not be using company time to pursue the complaint, which must be done on the employee's personal time."

Auman was missing something very important. The INL was not just 'any industry'; it was a DOE laboratory, operating in accordance with DOE regulations. Interestingly, Auman would later be promoted to the senior executive management team of DOE–ID.

In my opinion, it was totally inappropriate and improper for a DOE attorney to send me this email. It told me that DOE could not fulfill its obligation to provide independent oversight of BEA. It had only been a couple weeks since I filed my whistleblower complaint and DOE–Idaho was already taking the side of BEA.

During the next several weeks, I heard nothing more on this subject. I feared each day I went to work could be my last. There were moments of overwhelming despair and anguish, but I never lost hope. I knew that even if I was terminated, I would still have my faith, my family, and my friends.

***

I would later learn that a member of Mark Olsen's legal staff, Katherine Moriarty, had reported me for misuse of government equipment when she learned I had used my work phone and fax to request dismissal of my discrimination complaint with the Idaho Human Rights Commission. For me, it was egregiously wrong to launch an investigation of me based on my sending a fax to have a complaint dismissed. In my opinion it was simply a pretext to justify the ongoing harassment.

Chapter 25: Faith and Friendship

DURING THIS TIME of turmoil and uncertainty in my work life, I was also experiencing uncertainty about my church life. Since childhood, I had attended the same church, but now I was feeling a need to make a change. I came to believe that our family would benefit from attending a larger church with youth programs for Darius and Jasmine.

LaVonna and I prayed about this for weeks before deciding to visit other churches. The second church we visited was the First Church of the Nazarene. When the associate pastor began his message, he asked the congregation to turn to a specific passage in the Bible. The scripture was Acts 14:22: "They encouraged the believers to continue in the faith, reminding them that we must suffer many hardships to enter the Kingdom of God." This was the exact passage I had bookmarked in my Bible. I had read this passage just the day before.

At the end of his sermon the associate pastor asked for anyone going through hardship to stand up. LaVonna and I stood, along with a handful of others. Several church members came over and prayed for us. At the end of the service LaVonna and I knew that God had answered our prayers. We had found our new church home. A home that included two people who would become lifelong friends, Kirk and Joy Wilkie. Kirk was the younger brother of my high school friend, Craig. We had grown up in the same neighborhood, only a few blocks apart.

***

On the evening of Wednesday, August 27 our home phone rang. On the other end was a friend who called to let me know that a dear friend, Americus John-Lewis (AJ) was in critical condition at the local hospital. AJ was one of the few people with whom I had shared my recent troubles. He had been a big supporter, encourager, and confidant.

The next morning, I called in to work to let Doug know I would not be in the office because I needed to be with a friend at the hospital.

At the hospital I rode the elevator to the intensive care unit. The ICU was a controlled area and I had to press a button and identify myself prior to entering. The door opened and I walked down the hallway to AJ's room. Even lying in bed, AJ was an imposing figure. His six-foot nine-inch, nearly 300-pound frame seemed to barely fit in the bed.

When I saw his wife, Catherine, his son, Kevin, and his daughter Jennifer, there was extreme sadness in their eyes and grief on their faces. AJ was hooked up to life-saving devices and appeared to be in a deep sleep.

Catherine greeted me with a smile. "Hi, Dennis; it's so nice of you to come see AJ. He's in a coma, but we think he knows we are here."

I approached AJ, leaned over, squeezed his hand. "Hey, AJ, I'm here, man. I love you, my friend."

Throughout the morning I stayed with AJ and his family. While I was there, the doctor came into the room. The news wasn't good, but the doctor gave the family a little hope. Just before lunch, LaVonna stopped by to see AJ. She came in and gave everyone a big hug and words of encouragement.

A little later, I remembered something at work that required my attention. I apologized to Catherine, and promised to return as soon as possible.

When I got to my desk, the first thing I did was log onto my computer to check my email. My heart jumped when I saw an email from Torrance, the security investigator. The email said he needed to interview me again and that he wanted to do it this afternoon. I remembered the phone call from Torrance several weeks ago (July 13) when I was investigated for misuse of government equipment. Was I being investigated again? I replied and let him know I was on personal leave and would get back with him later to schedule the interview.

I returned to the hospital. Around 3:00 p.m. my cell phone rang. It was Torrance.

"Dennis, I need to interview you again. I need to ask you some follow-up questions from the interview. And there's something else I need to talk to you about."

I was livid about getting this call after emailing him that I was on personal leave. "So, have I been accused of some other misconduct and am being investigated again?"

"Dennis, has somebody told you there's another allegation against you?"

No one had told me anything, but his answer confirmed my suspicion. I decided to defer. I responded, "I'd rather not answer that question." I told Torrance I would call him back after my return to work and schedule the interview.

Later, this brief and seemingly innocuous phone conversation would become a major issue that BEA would use to justify taking further retaliation against me. However, at the moment I didn't care. AJ might be dying. The interview with Torrance would have to wait.

I stayed at the hospital until late afternoon. When it was time to leave, I explained to the family that LaVonna and I were flying out the next morning to visit her son James Williams in Fargo, North Dakota. We apologized for leaving at this time, but noted it had been planned for months. We told them we would call to see how AJ was doing. As I left the room I knew it might be the last time I would see him.

The next day, LaVonna and I arrived at the Fargo airport and rented a car. As we drove into the parking lot of the hotel, LaVonna's cell phone rang. We looked at each other as she handed me the phone. On the other end was AJ's son, Kevin. I knew it was bad news. His father had just died.

I don't remember what I said, but I remember Kevin thanking me for being a good friend to his dad. Tears welled up in my eyes as I felt the loss of a dear friend. LaVonna leaned over and held me as she gently kissed my cheek. We prayed for the family.

LaVonna and I enjoyed our visit with her son. It was good for me to see the love between them. James was a member of the National Guard and had returned from Iraq just in time for our wedding in May 2004. They hadn't seen each other since then.

AJ's funeral service took place the day after our return. The family asked me to say a few words and I was honored to do so. It was a beautiful service with many people including the mayor and other community leaders.

On September 2, 2006, the *Post Register's* front-page headline proclaimed "Local Activist Dies." The article was an excellent tribute to the impact AJ had on our community. My favorite part of the article was a quote from AJ. "I really believe that through love and prayer, we can overcome obstacles. It doesn't matter how high it is. If we want to, we can overcome."

Chapter 26: Cavalry

MY ATTENTION TURNED to my upcoming interview with Torrance. At this point I had zero trust in the system. I was convinced that Torrance was now part of a corrupt effort to retaliate against me for filing my whistleblower complaint. At my request, BEA agreed to allow my attorney, DeAnne Casperson, to be present during the interview. I went over and over in my mind trying to figure out what I had been accused of this time.

It had been almost two months since I was investigated for misuse of government equipment and I still didn't know the outcome. I knew that if Legal maintained it was inappropriate for me to write my whistleblower complaint on my computer I would likely be terminated.

On September 5, I sent an email to Olsen and Katherine Moriarty (lead attorney) and asked what they had decided.

The morning of the interview, September 6, 2006, I woke up early to have time to read my Bible and pray for God's protection. LaVonna gave me a kiss and said, "I will be praying for you; God will be with you."

I arrived at work and began preparing for the interview with Torrance. Shortly before the interview, I received an email from Katherine Moriarty in response to the inquiry I had sent the day before. Moriarty and Olsen finally made the right decision. It was within policy for me to write my whistleblower complaint on my work computer. I was relieved, but felt it was egregious to take fifty-five days to make a decision that many employees knew almost instinctively. I suspected they never would have informed me had I not sent them the email. To them, it was all a game. For me, it was the possibility of not being able to provide for my family.

It was mid-afternoon and time to go to Torrance's office and be interrogated once again. I sat at my desk and said a prayer before meeting DeAnne in the lobby of the Willow Creek building. We speculated as to what I had been accused of this time. Neither of us could come up with anything. Finally, we walked together to Torrance's office.

As we sat down, Torrance turned on his tape recorder. "Dennis, as you know, you are required to cooperate with this investigation," he began.

He informed me that the new allegation against me was filed by Eric Greenwade's manager, Patrick O'Leary — the same manager I had found guilty of unfair treatment just two short months previous. Management had retaliated against Eric for filing his complaint and now they were retaliating against me. They had filed a complaint with Legal that I had been biased in my investigation of Eric's allegation against them.

Now I knew just how vicious Eric's management team could be. And I suspected that Olsen and Benson were fully supportive of the decision to investigate me.

Torrance began the questioning by asking about the first allegation: misuse of government equipment. I asked him if he had seen the email from legal that stated writing my whistleblower complaint on my work computer was not a violation of policy. Torrance said he hadn't, so I handed him a copy.

He then asked, "Has anyone told you there was another allegation filed against you?"

"No."

"So, why did you refuse to answer this question when we talked on the phone?'

I laughed. "I wanted to keep you guessing and kind of level the playing field."

He chuckled and proceeded with his questioning. He focused on the report I had issued to Eric's management. I explained the process and protocols I used in conducting the investigation. The interview lasted approximately ninety minutes.

After leaving the interview, DeAnne and I discussed how it went. We expressed our disbelief that I was being investigated by Security for alleged bias.

"Dennis, you handled yourself very well."

"Thanks. I'm certain these two investigations are in direct response and retaliation for my filing the whistleblower complaint in June."

What made matters worse was the fact that Security was performing the investigations, the same division I had found guilty of misconduct in the Loren Mitchell matter in 2005. The motive for retaliation couldn't be more obvious. DeAnne agreed, but noted it was clear BEA was intent on coming after me. It was my opinion that my retaining an attorney made it less likely I would be terminated. They were put on notice that I intended to fight the fight to the end. My cavalry had arrived.

Chapter 27: Affirmations

I WAS SCHEDULED TO ATTEND the fall Employee Concerns Program Conference in Indianapolis, Indiana. Ironically, on the heels of having been investigated twice in the past few weeks, I would be representing BEA as the ethics officer. I left on September 11, 2006.

The third day of the conference included a breakout session with DOE. During the round table discussion, I mentioned that it took BEA senior management two months to decide an employee could use his computer to file a whistleblower complaint. Most expressed surprise that this was even debatable. "Of course, an employee can file a whistleblower complaint on his work computer," was the most common response.

I chose not to tell them I was the employee filing a whistleblower complaint. However, later in a private discussion with Billie Garde, I shared pertinent details of my complaint, specifically that I had been investigated twice over the past two months.

"Dennis, it's hard to believe any company would do this, but I tell you this, I'll be shocked if they decide to terminate you."

We spoke for over an hour. It felt good to have the support and encouragement of someone who knew what I was going through. At the end of our conversation she gave me her business card, which I tucked away in my wallet.

Upon returning from the conference, I decided to file an addendum to my whistleblower complaint. On September 19, 2006, it was filed. I alleged that BEA management had initiated the two investigations of me in retaliation for filing my whistleblower complaint.

As September wound to a close I was looking forward to my next business trip. On October 3, 2006, I drove to Salt Lake City, Utah for the annual Ethics Officer Conference. On the second day of the conference a speaker really grabbed my interest. He spoke about the challenges of being an ethics officer. I have never forgotten one of his comments. "Anyone who is or wants to be an ethics officer should be prepared to be fired. There are times when senior management doesn't want to hear the message; the messenger often becomes the scapegoat."

Yes, I was prepared to be fired, but I would fight until the end to protect my job, family, reputation, and integrity.

Chapter 28: Judgment Day

MONDAY, OCTOBER 16, 2006, I sat at my computer with the door to my office slightly ajar. At approximately 3:30 p.m., a shadow appeared in the doorway. The door swung open and Benson walked in. I glanced up and saw a document in his hand. My heart stopped. Was this the proverbial axe?

Benson grabbed a chair from the round table and placed it directly in front of my desk. He had a look of arrogance and coldness. The time had come.

"Dennis, you have been found guilty of serious misconduct." He shoved the discipline letter in front of me. In bold letters were the words: SUSPENSION WITHOUT PAY.

Benson read aloud the first paragraph. "Your failure to cooperate with an investigation by misleading an investigator; refusal to answer investigation questions regarding the unauthorized use of government computers and systems and the attendant inferred unauthorized use of government computers and systems; failure to follow company policies and protocols regarding an Employee Concerns investigation; failure to follow directions from BEA Office of General Counsel."

I sat there in horror and disbelief. I looked Benson in his stone-cold blue eyes and said nothing. I knew words would be futile and would probably be used against me.

Benson slowly rose to his feet. "Your suspension begins now; let's go."

I took a deep breath. On the wall next to my computer hung a poster that contained Bible scriptures and quotes from Dr. Martin Luther King. I read aloud scripture from Proverbs 10:9. "Whoever walks in integrity walks securely, but he who makes his ways crooked will be found out." I wanted these words to ring in Benson's head and lie silently in his heart. He had always taken such pride in his Mormon faith, and being good and kind. My hope was that somewhere deep inside he would recognize the crookedness of the path he had chosen for the past twenty months.

Benson followed closely behind as I walked down to the guard station near the front entrance. He took my INL badge and the keys to my office.

"I'll see you back here at the end of your week's suspension."

It felt as though I was having an out-of-body experience. I was watching someone be unjustly persecuted and humiliated. As I crossed the bridge heading to my car the feeling of betrayal was overwhelming. I sat in my car for what seemed like hours, but was probably only a few minutes. I prayed that God would help me through this.

With tears rolling down my cheeks and hands trembling I called LaVonna.

"Hi, Sweetheart, I've just been suspended without pay. I can't believe this is happening. I know I've done nothing wrong. How can this be happening?"

"I love you, the kids love you, and God loves you. We'll get through this."

***

Upon returning to work, I met Benson at the guard desk. The smirk on his face told me all I needed to know about the things to come. For the next few months, I was required to meet with him weekly to review my progress. I did everything that was outlined in my discipline letter. As such, the meetings went fairly well. Benson appropriately noted my good performance, though he couldn't hide his disdain. He took every opportunity to question and challenge my performance. He just couldn't find anything.

A couple of weeks after my return I filed another whistleblower complaint. I alleged that the suspension without pay was another act of retaliation.

The rest of the year was pretty uneventful. I performed a very thankless job to the best of my ability. Many of my friends and colleagues knew I had been disciplined and been given time off without pay. They also knew I had filed the whistleblower complaint. In spite of this, most remained my friends and regularly stopped by my office to visit and provide words of encouragement.

Chapter 29: Inaugural Dr. King Banquet

The African American Alliance hosted the first Dr. Martin Luther King Jr. banquet on January 20, 2007. Our keynote speaker was Dr. Walter Massey, president of Morehouse University. A few months prior, Morehouse was selected as the keeper of thousands of Dr. King's papers. Dr. Massey had once been the Laboratory Director for Argonne National Laboratories. Argonne National Laboratory West was located near Idaho Falls and as a result Massey had visited Idaho Falls several times during the 1990s.

The MC for the night was Karole Honas, longtime news anchor and friend of the AAA.

Mayor Jared Fuhriman opened the event with remarks and welcomed the more than 250 attendees. It was an amazing evening. Ladies wore their finest and men dressed in everything from tuxedos to Levi's (this is Idaho where boots and Stetsons are considered formal wear).

Dr. Massey gave a historical and memorable keynote address. His speech was titled, "A New Look at Dr. Martin Luther King Jr.: A Formula for Social Change in the 21st Century." Below are some excerpts from his speech:

Our challenge today is not desegregation as it was in the 1960s. And we can be proud — or at least grateful — that as a nation we have moved beyond separate water fountains and restrooms for coloreds and whites. But I think it is important to note here that desegregation, in and of itself, was not Dr. King's ultimate dream. It was much more than that. His vision was integration — a society where individuals live together and work together across racial lines.

In many ways, the mission of the Idaho Falls AAA — which is to initiate dialogue and contribute to the development of the community — can be viewed as a commitment to be engaged. Indeed, it is through dialogue that we begin to give shape to our hopes and dreams, and it is through sharing those dreams that we engage others in the process of change.

Because it is a fairly, but not exclusively, homogeneous racial, ethnic, and religious community, Idaho Falls has quite a number of opportunities to demonstrate the quality of empathy. There are minorities in this community — African American, Native Americans, and Hispanics, to be sure. Members of the Mormon church, although not a minority here, are minorities in America as a whole. No doubt they have had to endure prejudice in the face of ignorance about their religious beliefs, just as other minorities have had to endure prejudice in the face of ignorance about their racial and ethnic identities. To empathize is to embrace humanity — our own and each other's.

We can be assured that from an evolutionary perspective, Dr. King's ideas apply to our time, just as they did to his. And we can honor him best by taking on the challenge he left us to educate, engage, empathize, and effect a world's house that one day will be the kind of house that everyone can call home.

As I left the banquet, arm in arm with LaVonna, I felt honored and privileged to be a part of an event that was a tribute to my hero, Dr. Martin Luther King, Jr. I was proud of my community for a great turnout and overwhelming support.

The African American Alliance awarded three college scholarships to graduating African American students. The criteria included grade point average, educational plans, and personal narrative. One of the recipients was Jonathon Mitchell. Jonathon was the son of Loren Mitchell — the man who had been referred to as a scumbag and unworthy of working at the Idaho National Laboratory.

Chapter 30: I Refuse

THE MORNING OF MARCH 22, 2007, Benson told me he had scheduled a meeting for us that afternoon. When I entered his office, I was surprised to see a manager of Security, Joanie Pechtel. Benson began the meeting by discussing a case that I had turned over to Security five months ago. I found it exceedingly odd that this was the topic of conversation.

I couldn't believe what came next.

"Dennis, you must disclose the name of the employee who reported the allegation," Joan said.

I had never before been asked to disclose the name of a confidential reporting party. My temples began to throb and my chest felt heavy. I tried to explain why disclosing the person's name was wrong and how doing so would damage employee trust.

"You have to understand, I told the employee I would honor the request for confidentiality."

Benson's body stiffened and veins popped out on his forehead. I thought I could hear his teeth grind.

Joan's face turned beet red and her eyes bulged. She leaned toward me as if to intimidate me.

"Tell us the name. You don't have a choice!"

"I have never done so before and I don't intend to now."

We spent several minutes going back and forth. Benson and Joan continued to demand I disclose the name. I continued to defend my right and obligation to maintain confidentiality. It was clear this wasn't an argument I was going to win. Before leaving, I reiterated they were not going to get the name of the employee from me.

***

On November 2, 2006, I had received the following email.

"Dennis, there are many people who sit next to XXX, and we hear her on the phone all day long discussing political matters and campaigning. Could you please put a stop to it? Thanks, I'd like to remain anonymous."

On November 3 I replied, "Hi, after receiving your complaint I contacted BEA Security and informed them of this matter. They have done an initial review and would like to speak to you if you'd be willing to do so. They understand your desire to remain anonymous and thus have offered to have you make the call from my office phone so they won't know your identity. I stress it is totally up to you. Please get back to me."

"I don't have a problem using your phone. I'm not trying to get her fired, but I felt like it isn't my place to go to her directly and tell her how to do her job, so you were the best person I could think of."

The person accused of conducting political activity and campaigning was a former state legislator who had significant influence in the community and the state. I could understand why the person wanted to remain anonymous.

***

Now, here I was, five months later being asked by Security to disclose the name of someone who had specifically requested to remain anonymous.

The next day, March 23, I sent Benson an email. I stated my

belief that it was wrong to disclose the name. I wanted to ensure there was no ambiguity about what he and Security were asking me to do and what my position was.

On April 10, 2007, Benson sent me an email stating it was my obligation to find a resolution to Security's demand that I release the confidential name. Over the next few days, I contacted friends and colleagues with experience in the field of Employee Concerns and Ethics. I called a friend at a DOE National Laboratory back East. She informed me that there was only one occasion where she had been asked to disclose confidentiality. In retrospect, she said she shouldn't have done so, but management had convinced her it was okay. "Dennis, I would never do it again."

I also contacted Dan Robertson, Director of Employee Concerns for another contractor at the INL.

"Dennis, in more than twenty-five years of conducting investigations and managing employee concerns I have only been asked to break confidentiality once. And even then, I did so only after getting approval from the employee."

Dan helped me develop three viable options to offer in response to the Benson email. The options included: 1) Security provide me with the questions they needed answered and I would ask them of the employee 2) Let me ask the employee for permission 3) Refer the matter to BEA senior management inclusive of Art Clark or Grossenbacher. In Dan's and my opinion, these options would allow Security to move forward with their investigation without damaging the integrity of the Ethics Office.

That evening I spoke to LaVonna about the options.

She responded, "Dennis, I don't believe this will satisfy them. I don't even think this is the real issue. They are just trying to intimidate and threaten you."

After a restless night's sleep, I awoke knowing what I had to do. I told LaVonna I could not in good conscience disclose the name of the employee.

"I trust your decision, my love."

Upon arriving at work, I sent Benson an email. I informed him that I would not release the name. I communicated the three options I believed would assist Security in their investigation. I hoped that reason would prevail and this ugly situation would come to an end. However, I couldn't help but think that LaVonna was right. This really wasn't about disclosing the confidential name.

Chapter 31: A Friend's Betrayal

FOR SEVERAL DAYS, there was no response to my email. I only saw Benson occasionally, but we never spoke, not even 'hello.' I was getting very little sleep and had lost my appetite. Sometimes just walking down the hall was exhausting.

Finally, on April 16, Benson darkened my doorway. "Dennis, come over to my office now."

Sitting at the wooden rectangular desk was Tom Middleton, Joan's boss, and director of INL Security. Tom was also my neighbor and someone I considered a friend. In fact, in 1998 he had testified at my divorce hearing. During the child custody phase, he testified that he knew me well, that our children were good friends, that I was a good parent and a person of integrity.

My supposed friend began the meeting. "Dennis, you must and will tell my investigator, Dyanna, the name of the confidential employee." For the next several minutes Tom pontificated about the responsibility and authority of the Security division.

Benson chimed in, "Dennis, it is your obligation to tell Security the name."

I was alarmed by their arrogance and sense of absolute authority. I had no doubt they had already obtained the concurrence and approval of Mark Olsen. I was also certain they had taken into account that I was African American, and hence had also consulted with Arantza Zabala, Diversity manager. The office that was supposed to protect the rights of minorities was now part of a corrupt effort to destroy the career of a previously well-known and well respected African American — me.

As they spoke, I just listened and watched.

Finally, I responded. "Tom, you know me, you know I will not violate my professional or personal ethics. Your investigators don't understand BEA or DOE policies; if they did, they wouldn't be asking me to disclose the name."

"My investigators know what they are doing and you will give us the name."

"Dennis, I'm with Tom on this," Benson interjected.

"So, to be clear, are you directing me to disclose the name?"

Benson replied, "I'm not directing you to but you have an obligation to help Security proceed with the investigation.

I walked back to my office and closed the door. I looked at the quotes on my wall. Dr. Martin Luther King said: "The ultimate measure of a man is not where he stands in times of comfort and convenience, but where he stands in times of challenge and controversy."

I knew where I was going to stand.

On April 24, I was again called into a meeting with Benson and Middleton. Benson shoved a letter in front of me. Benson referred to the last page, "You have until 9:00 a.m. tomorrow morning to provide the name of the employee."

I sat there in disbelief. In spite of my efforts to find a workable solution, BEA was forcing me to violate confidentiality. To make matters worse, I was being given less than twenty-four hours to make a career and life-changing decision.

I looked across the table at Benson and Middleton. "You both know me well enough to know what I'm going to do."

As I rose to leave, my heart was pounding as though it would come through my shirt.

I paused in the doorway, turned, and looked at Middleton. Through clenched teeth I said, "You're doing a great job as Security Director."

Middleton had only recently been named director of Security. Yes, I was being sarcastic, but I was also trying to make a point. Little did I know that this single comment, made out of frustration, would come back to haunt me.

I returned to my office and prepared an email to Grossenbacher and other senior managers. I needed to get them to understand the gravity of this situation. I was trying to save my job and at the same time keep the company from doing something that could damage employee and public trust. At 8:34 p.m. I hit the send key. As I turned off my computer and closed the door, I knew this would likely be the last time I would be able to call this my office.

Chapter 32: The Decision

The drive home seemed to take forever. It was as though everything was in slow motion. My emotions were running rampant, my thoughts raced, and my body reacted to the stress and duress of the day. As I pulled into the garage, I looked in the rearview mirror and saw the Middleton house across the street. I felt sick as I realized that my one-time friend was now a threat to my career and my ability to provide for my family.

Upon entering the house, I greeted the kids as though nothing was wrong. Ziggy came running and jumped in my lap. As I prepared dinner, I kept watching the clock, anxious for LaVonna to come home. When she arrived, I greeted her with a smile and a kiss, but I was sure she knew something was wrong.

Later that evening, after the kids had gone to bed, we finally had a chance to talk. I could see the pain on LaVonna's face as I told her the story. Until now, I had been able to provide us with a beautiful home and opportunities I had only dreamed about as a child. Now, our financial security was at risk.

"Dennis, you've already done more than should be expected of anyone. Maybe now is the time to think more about yourself," LaVonna gently offered.

"I know, Sweetheart. I need to be sure that I'm doing the right thing for the right reason." We talked until almost midnight. We prayed for peace, comfort, understanding, and direction.

I awoke before sunrise and cuddled up next to LaVonna. She turned around and looked at me. "I can't do it, Sweetheart; it's about my integrity. I just can't do it," I whispered.

"I know, I've always known; everything is going to be okay."

I decided not to leave for work until 9:00 a.m., the official deadline for me to give Security the name. I sat in our bedroom listening to gospel music. The song that played was a spiritual that gave me encouragement and hope. I straightened my tie and adjusted my suit coat.

I chose to dress in a suit and tie for two reasons. First, as the old saying goes, "look good, feel good." Second, I hoped to plant the seed in Benson's mind that I was preparing to speak to the media. This might create enough fear in his mind not to fire me today. I left the house knowing I was doing the right thing and I had LaVonna's love and support.

As I entered the building, I greeted my friend Blaine, the security guard. I rode the escalator to the second floor and walked to Benson's office. He was standing by his computer. I stood in the doorway.

"Doug, I just got to work."

"Did you give the name to Security?"

"No, I did not. When will I know my punishment?"

"By the end of the day."

"You need to make sure Grossenbacher is made aware of your decision. The outcome could cause harm to the company and result in public embarrassment."

I was already contemplating going to the press if I were to be terminated. In my pocket I had the phone numbers of Karol Honas, other news anchors, and the *Post Register*. The headline I envisioned, "BEA Fires Ethics Officer for Refusing to Violate Confidentiality."

The rest of the story would include the fact that I was the president of the African American Alliance. I would note that a state legislator was being investigated for misconduct. And finally, that Security had been investigating the issue for the past six months with no resolution. Never before had a case taken six months to investigate. If such a story were to be published, it would be an embarrassment to BEA, Battelle Corporate, and of course, John Grossenbacher. I didn't want to take such a drastic action, but I was prepared to do so to protect my job and my family.

"Doug, I'll be in and out of the office today, but I'll be back to find out my punishment."

I went to my office and called LaVonna. I told her what Benson had said and that I was going to try to meet with our pastor, Bob Sherwood, and then try to meet with my attorney, DeAnne Casperson. I called Bob's office and told the receptionist it was extremely important that I meet with him. I was relieved when she said he could meet with me at 1 p.m. I then called DeAnne and told her what was going on. She told me to stop by her office after meeting with Bob.

At 10:25 a.m. I heard the beep of my computer letting me know I had received an email. I looked up at the monitor. The email was from Richard Cohen, the person from DOE Headquarters investigating my whistleblower complaint. I stared at the computer screen. My stomach churned. If the report found in BEA's favor it would likely embolden them enough to terminate me by the end of the day. On the other hand, if the report found in my favor there was the likelihood that I would remain employed and even possibly remain in my job.

My heart pounded as I read the several page document. When I got to the end I just sat there. I had neither won nor lost.

The report concluded that the case would proceed to a formal hearing and be decided by a DOE Hearing Officer. I breathed a sigh of relief. I knew that the prospect of a hearing would make BEA think twice about terminating me today.

I arrived at the church office promptly at 1 p.m. "Hello, Carolyn," I said to the office administrator. Hearing my voice, Bob came out to greet me. Bob had a real heart to serve and a genuine compassion for people. As we sat down at the table I tried to put on a brave front. I began by telling him the events that had unfolded over the past two years. I then described the stress of the past twenty-four hours.

"Bob, I believe I made the right choice, but I don't want to lose my job. I need to be able to take care of my family. I don't understand why this is happening to me." By this time, tears were rolling down my face. When I looked up, I could see Bob's eyes were wet as well.

"Dennis, God loves you. Your faith will help you get through this. I believe you made the right and just decision. If they fire you, I'm sure many companies would love to hire someone like you."

At the end of our conversation Bob prayed for me. His words comforted me beyond my expectations. We parted with a big hug.

Bolstered by my visit with Bob I drove across the river to DeAnne's office. We met for about an hour. She assessed my legal standing and the strength of my case.

"Dennis, it is unlikely they will terminate you today, but you can never tell."

I arrived back to work around 4 p.m. When I turned on my computer, I saw that Benson had sent me an email at 3:45. I opened the email. BEA had decided to postpone making a decision. I still had a job, for now. I felt numb, kind of like a death row inmate must feel when he receives a stay of execution. I was glad I had a chance for another day, but the guillotine continued to hang over my head.

Chapter 33: The Big Guns

THREE DAYS LATER, April 27, 2007, I called the DOE Hearing Officer, Valerie Adeyeye. I told her about BEA directing me to disclose a confidential source and my refusal to do so. I expressed my fear that I could be terminated at any time.

"Please schedule the hearing as soon as possible," I asked.

"I'll contact BEA and try to schedule the hearing for early June."

I was thrilled at the prospect of having my day in court so soon. Until now, I had only consulted with DeAnne Casperson. I didn't intend to have her represent me for the hearing because I knew it would cost a lot of money. Plus, I felt fully confident in my ability to represent myself.

"Ms. Adeyeye, I plan to represent myself at the hearing."

"That's totally acceptable but I strongly suggest you consider obtaining an attorney."

That evening LaVonna and I discussed the phone call with Adeyeye.

"I think it would be wise to take Adeyeye's advice."

"I know, but I've participated in a hearing before. I know how it works. And I'm really good at researching, analyzing data, and presenting strong oral arguments. I know I can do this."

Using much kinder words than the axiom, *A man who is his own attorney has a fool for a client,* LaVonna was able to convince me that it would be wise to retain counsel.

The next day we met with DeAnne. Because she knew me and had provided advice since June 2006, she agreed to take my case.

"Dennis, I'm happy to take your case. But I'm a little concerned because I have no experience with DOE whistleblower cases."

"It doesn't matter because I do. I've even testified in an INL whistleblower case."

"Okay, but you need to understand it will likely cost at least thirty thousand dollars."

LaVonna and I looked at each other as our jaws dropped. We knew that if we prevailed BEA would have to pay the costs but if we lost this would create an incredible hardship on us. By the time we left her office, there was no doubt that we needed her on our team, no matter the cost.

On May 10, after coming home from a long and stressful day, I picked up the mail and noticed a letter with a return address from Seattle, Washington: Halvorson Saunders & Willner, PLLC. The letter was my notification that this law firm would be representing BEA, in association with Mark Olsen and his staff. It surprised me that BEA would be willing to spend what could be upwards of hundreds of thousands of dollars to defend a DOE whistleblower case.

Under DOE Code of Federal Regulations 708, BEA was at little-to-no financial loss. Whistleblowers are not able to gain financially. The only monies available to a DOE whistleblower are those that are taken from them such as loss of job, loss of merit increase, suspension, and attorney costs. I had never heard of a DOE contractor retaining outside legal representation for a whistleblower case, and certainly never at the INL.

Obviously, BEA understood the risk to their reputation and would spare no cost to make sure they didn't lose. The stage was set. Me, with a small-town local attorney vs. BEA and the big guns from Washington.

Chapter 34: The Angry Black Man

ON A BEAUTIFUL, WARM DAY in May I received a phone call from Ms. Toni Vandel, BEA Diversity Specialist.

"Dennis, I need to speak with you tomorrow."

"What for?"

"Management has tasked me to conduct an investigation."

"I want to know why."

"I'll have to get back to you."

Later that day, I learned via email that I was being investigated for "behavior and/or actions in the meeting held on April 24 with Benson and Middleton."

The following day I sat at my desk and prayed as I prepared to walk downstairs and meet with Vandel. When I arrived, Arantza Zabala was seated at the table. Vandel sat on the opposite side with pad and pencil.

We sat at the round table with Zabala nearest me asking the questions and Vandel on the far side of the table taking notes. I knew both of them very well, having worked with them for many years. In fact, Zabala and I had conducted interviews together in the past.

Zabala began, "Doug Benson and Tom Middleton have asked us to investigate you. They allege that you did not treat them with dignity and respect in the April 24 meeting."

"I don't think it was fair for them to put me in that situation. I was intimidated and harassed to disclose a confidential source and now I'm the one being investigated? This is wrong."

Zabala cited several statements I allegedly made that demonstrated I hadn't treated Benson and Middleton respectfully. As she read each one, I replied with "okay," acknowledging that I understood what she was saying. There was only one statement that I admitted was less than professional. This was when I remarked, "Tom, you are doing a great job as Security director." I felt as though it really didn't matter what I said or didn't say to Vandel and Zabala.

It was clear to me that BEA wasn't interested in the truth. They were intent on continuing the pattern of intimidation, abuse, and retaliation. Since filing the whistleblower complaint on June 1, 2006, this was the third time I had been investigated for alleged misconduct. The idea that I would be investigated for not being nice to Benson and Middleton was absurd. They put me in an impossible situation, then portrayed me as the 'angry Black man.'

***

Three more weeks passed and I still hadn't been told what disciplinary action would be taken against me for not disclosing the name. I continued to perform my job to the best of my ability.

On June 9, I received an anonymous letter that contained a very serious allegation. The letter alleged that BEA had been promoting and unfairly compensating the spouse of Idaho Congressman Mike Simpson. Supposedly, this was being done to gain favor with Simpson and thereby improve INL's posture in Washington D.C.

This was not the first time INL had received an allegation like this. In the late 90s I had investigated a similar complaint and found no merit to the allegation. Nonetheless, I believed we had an obligation to at least review the current complaint. Later that afternoon I gave the letter to Benson, who in turn notified Middleton.

Middleton responded via email noting that because a similar issue had been addressed previously no further action was warranted. Middleton expressed his displeasure that we would even consider investigating this anonymous complaint. To Benson's credit, he wrote back to Middleton and told him that a meeting should be convened as soon as possible so that we could agree upon a path forward.

Benson tasked me with scheduling a meeting with Security, Legal, Human Resources, and me. I scheduled the meeting for the afternoon of June 14, 2007. Little did I know that this would be the last I would ever hear or know anything about this issue.

Chapter 35: The Verdict

ON JUNE 13, 2007, Benson stopped in the doorway of my office. "Come to my office now."

When I arrived Zabala was seated at the table. "Take a seat, Dennis."

This was the moment. My heart raced and I felt tightness in my chest. I didn't have the chance to pray prior to the meeting. I remained silent. Benson glared at me as he peered over his reading glasses. Zabala pushed her hair back from her face and leaned forward with an exaggerated sense of authority.

I sat across from Zabala and diagonally from Benson. I took a deep breath. I noticed a letter in Benson's hand. He placed it on the table and pushed it toward me.

"Management has decided to remove you from the Ethics Office.

"One of the reasons is your failure to treat Tom and me with respect and, as you see on page two, your failure to disclose the name of the confidential employee."

Although I was hurting and angry, I chose not to argue or defend myself. I knew it would do no good, and that anything I might say could be used against me.

"Your removal is effective immediately; let's go to your office. You can pack up your personal stuff."

When we got to my office, Zabala stood in the doorway and Benson sat down. They watched as I removed pictures from the wall and gathered personal items such as birthday cards, cups, and awards. I paused as I picked up the family photo on my desk. I felt numb as I pondered how I would explain to Jasmine and Darius why I was no longer the ethics officer. I had often told them how I much I loved my job because I was able to help people. They were both so proud of me.

Benson interrupted my thought. "Dennis, let's go. I'll introduce you to your new manager."

"No, thank you, I'm going home. I can meet him tomorrow."

Benson seemed annoyed, but he didn't challenge me.

I caught the escalator down to the lobby. As I walked past the Security desk, I remembered taking this same path when I was suspended for three days in October 2006. But this time when I return, I will no longer be the INL ethics officer.

I sat in the parking lot. My body shook and my head ached. I don't remember what I was thinking; I felt a deep sense of loss and despair. I decided not to call LaVonna. I wanted to tell her in person.

It was a sunny day, so I drove along the river on my way home. Many times before, I had driven by the river as a way of unwinding and calming my spirit. I tried to grasp the gravity of what had just happened and what life would look like in the future.

By the time I arrived home, I was composed but still a little unsteady. The kids and Ziggy were playing in the backyard.

"Hey kids, I'm home. I'll be out later; I need to take care of some things in the house."

When LaVonna came home I greeted her with a hug.

"Sweetheart, I'm no longer the ethics officer. Benson removed me today. It hurts so much."

"I can't believe they did this to you; this is so wrong."

"I know; I feel like going across the street and banging on Tom's door. I feel like going to Benson's house and punching him in the face. This is so damn unfair!"

"It's okay, babe; everything's going to be okay. I love you and the kids love you."

After dinner, we decided it was time to tell Darius and Jasmine.

We walked into the family room. They were seated on the couch watching TV. LaVonna and I sat across from them on the loveseat. I turned off the TV.

"Hey kids, I need to talk to you for a minute. You know how much I love my job," I paused. "Well, as of today I am no longer the ethics officer."

"Why, Dad; what happened?"

"Well, as I've taught you, keeping your word is one of the most important things you can do. I kept a promise to an employee who asked me not to tell anyone his or her name. Doug Benson and Tom Middleton tried to make me disclose the name. When I refused, Doug removed me from my job. Some of these things have been going on for more than a year, but I didn't tell you because I didn't want you to be worried. I love you guys so much."

"We love you, too, Dad."

I knew at this moment that no matter what happened, I would always have my faith, family, and friends. Nothing was more important.

Chapter 36: Integrity

THE NEXT MORNING I was mentally and emotionally prepared to return to work and meet my new boss. I was anxious to find out what my new job duties would be and to begin building a good relationship with my new management team.

I stopped by Benson's office. As it turned out, my new manager's office was just down the hall from my old office. Doug introduced me to my new boss, Ed Anderson, and left without any explanation. Also present was Ed's boss, Deb Tate. Both looked very uncomfortable, but they did their best to make me feel comfortable. I shook their hands and told them I looked forward to the new challenge.

Deb began, "Our division is called Engineering Services. Our mission is to provide engineering services to divisions throughout the INL." After several minutes of describing the organization of the department, the discussion turned to my job description.

"Dennis, your title will be Management Systems Process Lead. You will report directly to Ed and your role will be to provide engineering support to engineers and managers."

It was clear to me that I didn't have the experience or education needed to be successful in this role or organization.

"Ed, may I see the written job description for this job?"

Ed opened up his folder and handed it to me. As I suspected, the requirements read, "bachelor's degree plus fifteen years or advanced degree and thirteen years of extensive engineering experience, exposure and command of engineering design, analysis and configuration management process and principles."

"I have zero engineering experience and my degree is in business."

Ed slumped in his chair and Deb dropped her pen on the desk. It was as though I had told them I was from another planet.

"What makes you think I'm qualified for this job?"

"Well, you must be very good because you're currently in a senior level position."

"Yes, I am very good at what I do, but I am not an engineer and don't have the required qualifications."

"Dennis, prior to this, we didn't have any knowledge about your experience or education, but I will commit to do whatever is necessary to give you a fair chance to succeed."

"And I commit to being the best I can be to make this work."

Ed walked me over to my new office. It was a cubicle with a window that faced one of the equipment buildings. I had the feeling that this was a not-so-subtle message on the part of Benson and others. I had gone from a comfortable private office to a cubicle where everyone could see and hear me.

A couple of days later, Ed presented me with a new position description. The job duties were revised and the qualifications modified. The job wouldn't be challenging or rewarding, but it afforded me an opportunity to succeed. Ed had been true to his word. A man of integrity.

***

On June 19, 2007, I learned that a long time and well-respected senior manager, Dr. Jim Lake, was retiring from BEA. Dr. Lake had been a senior manager for the past ten years. In addition, he had served a term as the president of the American Nuclear Society. Jim and I worked several issues together and we shared a mutual respect. I suspected that his retirement was related to the fact that BEA had previously replaced him as director of Nuclear Science & Technology. I was sorry he was retiring. Jim was one of only three BEA senior managers who knew my long history of contributions to the laboratory. Jim was a person with great integrity.

I sent an email to Jim thanking him for his ethical leadership.

He responded, "Thanks, Dennis; you've been wonderful to work with, and you've made it easy for us managers to do the right thing."

Receiving such a message from someone of Dr. Lake's stature was humbling, but also rewarding.

I also sent an email to Kathryn McCarthy to inform her of my reassignment.

"Dennis, I'm so sorry to hear this. I have nothing but the highest regards for the work you did in the Ethics Office. Makes me wonder what kind of person they've replaced you with (seems like they're not looking for someone with high ethical standards). Please keep the faith — I still have to believe things will work out in the end."

The next day I sent an email to senior manager, Dr. Harold Blackman. Earlier Blackman had invited me to be a member of the INL Institutional Review Board. The Board was chartered with ensuring that any INL research or experiments that involved human subjects met the highest ethical standards and protected the rights and dignity of the subjects. I was honored by the request and had gladly accepted.

But now I had a responsibility and obligation to inform Blackman that I had been removed from the Ethics Office. I anticipated that with this knowledge, he might feel compelled to ask me to resign as a member of the Board.

Instead, he asked me to remain on the Board. In Harold's twenty plus years at INL he had always demonstrated the highest integrity.

Olsen, Middleton, Zabala, Benson and others had tried to beat me down, humiliate me, and destroy my reputation. But they had failed. No one could take away that which God had given me.

On June 25, 2007, I attended Dr. Lake's retirement party. Senator Larry Craig's Idaho Falls regional director, Knut Meyerin, read a letter that had been entered into the Congressional record by Senator Craig. The letter acknowledged Dr. Lake for his great contributions to the laboratory and to nuclear energy. I had met Knut earlier in the year at Skyline High School. He and I were members of the Skyline Character Education Coalition (SCEC). The goal of SCEC was to promote student awareness of the importance of character and integrity. We implemented a program to reward and recognize students who exhibited the highest standards of ethical conduct. It didn't matter what their grade point average was or if they were great at sports. What mattered were values such as kindness, honesty, integrity, and compassion.

At the end of Lake's retirement party, I visited with Knut.

"Dennis, how have you been doing? How's the job going?"

"I'm doing okay, but I discovered some unethical actions by management. I filed a whistleblower complaint with DOE. And since then, I have been harassed, intimidated, and removed as ethics officer."

"You know, Dennis, it's not unusual for someone like you to report an issue and then be retaliated against. Please send me more information about your situation."

I later sent Knut an email with a link to my whistleblower complaint that was on the DOE website. The next day I received an email from Knut: "Hi, Dennis, yes, I did find it and downloaded the information. If you feel my presence at your hearing will help, let me know."

I was honored that a representative from the office of a United States senator was willing to attend my hearing as a way of showing his support. I replied, "I think it would help and I would love for you to attend."

Chapter 37: Hear Ye, Hear Ye

ON JUNE 27, two days after talking to Knut, I received a call.

"Hi, Dennis, my name is Paul Menser, a reporter with the *Post Register*. I have a copy of your complaint from the DOE website; my editor has asked me to write a story."

"How do you even know about this?"

"Well, my editor gave me the copy and asked me to do a story," he repeated.

I was sure that Knut had notified the *Post Register* of my complaint and had provided the copy.

At this point I was not comfortable speaking to the press. I had heard too many stories about how information is often misrepresented by the media. With this thought in mind, I kept my answers brief. I focused on the misconduct I reported and the retaliatory actions including the intimidation, low performance appraisal, and being removed from the Ethics Office.

The next morning, there it was on the front page of the *Post Register*. "INL Whistleblower turns to DOE to get complaints heard."

The story included the fact that I had uncovered problems in the Security division and had filed a whistleblower complaint in June 2006. It further stated that DOE Idaho had dismissed my complaint, but that the DOE Office of Hearings and Appeals reinstated the complaint. Overall, the story was accurate and balanced.

One piece of the article caught my attention. It contained a quote from Steve Kohn, president of the National Whistleblowers Association, based in Washington, D.C.

Kohn said the administrative path Patterson is following was designed by DOE to keep its employees in the dark about the better remedy available from the Department of Labor. Number one you want independence. Whistleblower cases can get politicized very fast, and DOE and DOE contract managers are very close when it comes to matters like this.

In my opinion, Kohn was absolutely correct. I had already experienced this when DOE Idaho attorney, Evan Auman, took the side of Mark Olsen in July 2006. And again when DOE–Idaho dismissed my complaint the same month.

I was glad that my complaint against BEA was now public. Perhaps now Grossenbacher would intervene and try to resolve this matter. Maybe he would realize he wasn't getting the truth from his management team.

Chapter 38: Beyond Unbelievable

THE HEARING OFFICER, Valerie Adeyeye, had rescheduled the whistleblower hearing to begin August 21, 2007, instead of early June. She encouraged both sides to consider using mediation, with the possibility of avoiding a trial. Of course, BEA quickly jumped at the opportunity. I didn't like the idea because mediation would only address issues such as my lost merit, job title, and suspension without pay. For me, the more important issue was getting my day in court so that the truth would be known. This would likely compel BEA to make fundamental changes to the work environment such that INL employees would not be punished for raising issues and employees would feel valued and respected.

After discussing this with LaVonna and consulting with DeAnne, I decided to participate in the mediation.

We quickly learned that although BEA wanted to mediate, they certainly didn't want to mediate in good faith. BEA conditioned the offer to mediate by stating unequivocally that they would not even consider reinstating me as ethics officer.

The morning of the mediation session, I arrived at DeAnne's office at 9 a.m. She directed me to the conference room. I had spent many hours in this room over the past several months. It was a large room with a great view of the Snake River. She left me there and said she would return when the BEA team arrived.

BEA was late. The clock ticked slowly; finally the door opened. DeAnne walked in with two BEA representatives. The first was Arantza Zabala, the same person who had investigated me in May. The second was BEA senior attorney, Katherine Moriarty, the person who had requested the investigation of me in June of 2006. I found it exceedingly poor judgment of BEA to select two individuals who were part of the retaliation to participate in the mediation. In my opinion, this was a recipe for failure.

The mediator was an older fellow. He slowly shuffled to his chair on the other side of the conference table and struggled a bit to get comfortable in the chair. He was clearly one who had enjoyed too many good meals. He opened his briefcase and flipped through a large stack of documents. I observed him carefully in order to get a sense of who he was and how he might conduct the session. He reminded me of an old country lawyer. He had the mannerism and style of TV's Matlock. He began by explaining the mediation process and the expectations.

The morning and first part of the afternoon was spent with everyone in the same room discussing facts, disagreeing at times, and positioning for the latter part of the mediation. During the discussion of one my alleged acts of misconduct the mediator said, "This is really trivial and blown way out of proportion." I was certain this didn't sit well with Zabala or Moriarty.

By late afternoon he had DeAnne and me, and Zabala and Moriarty go to separate rooms. He explained that he would be shuttling between the two rooms in an effort to come to an agreement.

During the next several hours, offers and counter offers were sent across the two rooms. As the clock approached 9 p.m. the sun was beginning to set and I was exhausted. We had been at this nonstop for twelve hours.

It appeared as though we might reach a resolution. As we got closer to agreement, I began to feel nauseous, like I might throw up. I realized that if we were to reach a settlement agreement, the past two years would have been for naught.

BEA was not willing to acknowledge any wrongdoing. They were simply trying to make the issues go away. There would be no changes in the work environment and no one would know what really happened.

Finally, around 11 p.m., DeAnne made our final offer.

Moriarty responded, "We don't have the authority to sign off on it. We'll present the offer to senior management, but we will not recommend it be approved."

Frustrated and exhausted, I left the building and drove home.

LaVonna and the kids met me at the door. Before I said a word, they knew from my expression that the fight wasn't over. Slowly, I began telling them what it was like to spend the entire day and most of the night trying to resolve things. I told them how hard it was to have to tell the story and relive all the feelings and emotions. It was well past midnight before we all went to bed. After a long hard day, it was so good to have the love and support of my family.

The next day BEA made a counter offer that was totally unacceptable. I respectfully declined.

I told DeAnne to contact BEA and extend my best and final offer. I would agree to a resolution if BEA would: 1) pay attorney fees, 2) remove all discipline from my file and reimburse me for the three days off without pay, 3) assign me to a new job comparable to my previous position, and 4) award me a 4 percent retroactive merit pay increase.

Almost immediately I regretted making the offer for the same reasons as before. Settling would not result in any changes in the work environment and the only person helped was me. In addition, I didn't trust that Zabala and Moriarty would find a suitable position for me. The last time they found me a job I got stuck being a make-believe engineer.

That evening I discussed my reservations with LaVonna.

"I understand, but I think you have to honor the offer if BEA accepts it."

"I know, and I will. I hope they turn it down."

The next day my phone rang.

"Dennis, BEA accepts your offer, with one exception. BEA will only give you a 3 percent raise. They say you have to accept more responsibility."

I was dumbfounded. Why on earth would BEA risk hundreds of thousands of attorney fees, and possible public embarrassment, when they could reach a settlement for almost nothing? It was beyond unbelievable.

"DeAnne, tell BEA I decline the offer. Tell them we'll see them at the hearing."

"Dennis, I'm surprised you're declining over the paltry sum of 1 percent."

"I want my day in court."

"Okay, I'll let them know."

The following morning, DeAnne called me. She sounded troubled and distressed.

"Dennis, I just got a call from the mediator. You and I need to talk. I need you to come down to my office."

"Sure, I'll be right down." I knew something was very wrong. I turned off my computer and headed downtown.

I entered her office and sat down at the large wooden table. The look on her face told me this was not good.

"Dennis, the call from the mediator was something I've never experienced before. I may be wrong, but he seemed to be pressuring me to get you to settle. He said that in his opinion if we were to lose, you might pursue legal action against me."

My jaw clenched and my hands trembled. It felt like everything was falling apart. If my attorney was having doubts, how could I win my case? Had Mark Olsen contacted the mediator and influenced him to intimidate DeAnne? The mediator was a retired judge from Boise. I doubted that even Olsen would have the audacity to take such a high-risk maneuver.

"DeAnne, you know I would never do that to you. The reason I want to pursue this is so that no other employee will have to go through what I've been through. I believe that going to trial will get everything out in the open."

"Dennis, I get it. I'm with you. Thank you for coming down and talking to me."

A few weeks later I was in DeAnne's office preparing for the trial when she received a phone call from Mark Olsen. His message: "Tell Dennis, if it's simply a matter of money, we can resolve this without having a hearing."

"DeAnne, tell Olsen it was never about money. I want my day in court."

The Hearing Officer scheduled the hearing to convene on Tuesday, November 27. She estimated the trial would take four days.

Chapter 39: Moving and Running

When LaVonna and I married in 2004 we had moved into my home. Now, we had decided it was time to find a home together. During the course of the summer we looked at many homes, trying to find just the right one for us and for Darius and Jasmine. Finally, in late July we found 'the one.' It was a beautiful modern home with a view of the golf course, a koi fish pond, and a waterfall. The vaulted ceilings created a panoramic view. The family room was ideal for family gatherings and holiday extravaganzas. This would be our forever home. When we told family and friends, some were quite concerned about the timing of our move. Buying a new home with the upcoming whistleblower trial seemed risky and impulsive. Nevertheless, LaVonna and I stepped out in faith. We moved in at the end of the month.

***

Around this same time, I was looking for opportunities to help others. For the past several years I had considered running for public office. The more I read the papers the more I became convinced that now was the time. The Idaho Falls City Council had experienced some rather embarrassing episodes. In fact, one of the council members had disclosed allegations of misconduct on the part of two city division directors.

LaVonna and I had several heart-to-heart discussions about me running for a council seat. She expressed reservations. Her biggest concern was the impact on our family at a time when so much was going on in our lives.

Eventually, we agreed this would be a positive thing for us and for the community. We believed it was time for a change in Idaho Falls. The theme for my campaign would be, "A Voice for Everyone."

On August 12, 2007, I officially declared my candidacy for a seat on the Idaho Falls City Council. I entered the race having no prior political experience. However, I was confident that my ethics background, education, and reputation would make me a strong candidate. A big worry was that my pending whistleblower complaint against the area's largest employer could work against me. I also considered the fact that I was Black and non-Mormon. But in the final analysis, I decided that those were some of the very reasons I needed to run. In Idaho Falls' 143-year history there had never been a Black on the city council.

LaVonna agreed to be my treasurer. Two of our first campaign volunteers were our friends Kirk and Joy Wilkie.

We spent long hours going door-to-door and talking with people. My greatest pleasure from campaigning was the opportunity to listen to the concerns of others. Occasionally, I met someone who knew my parents or one of my siblings. Without fail, they told me good things about my family.

One of the unique experiences was "Live Wire," hosted by the *Post Register*. Live Wire gave citizens an opportunity to ask questions and make comments. I was asked which of the presidential candidates I most admired and whose ideas aligned with mine. I paused and thought about not answering the question. I knew that if I answered truthfully it could damage my chances. Nonetheless, I answered, "Barack Obama." I had already become a strong supporter of Obama and was hopeful he would be our first African American president.

Chapter 40: One More Time

ON OCTOBER 23 LaVonna and I completed our scheduled campaign route and left for work. The day was pretty much like any other, but as the lunch hour approached, I received a call from Toni Vandel, an employee of Zabala's.

"Dennis, you need to come to Arantza's office. Torrance has lodged a complaint against you."

"What am I accused of this time?"

"You'll find out when you get here."

Over the next several hours, I tried to figure out what Torrance could be complaining about. The last time I saw him was approximately a month ago. We had exited the men's room near Vandel's office. Torrance was ahead of me as we walked toward the main lobby. As we approached the escalator, I decided to ask Torrance a question. I wanted to know if, and how long, they kept the tape recordings of Security interviews. He had recorded me twice in 2006 and the whistleblower hearing was coming up.

I had walked behind him for a short distance, waiting for an opportune time to speak to him. As he entered the cubicle area, just north of the escalator, he stopped to talk to a colleague. Seeing he was occupied, I decided not to ask him the question. I turned around and went back to my office. It was unfathomable that this incident could be the source of my being investigated again.

Zabala and Vandel were seated at a round table when I entered. Zabala began the interview.

"Torrance has formally charged you with following him with the intent to intimidate him. Did you follow Torrance about a month ago?"

"Yes, but only to ask him a question."

"Torrance has alleged that you intended to intimidate him."

I could tell by the tone of Arantza's voice and her mannerisms that she believed Torrance and discounted what I was saying.

I looked across the table at Zabala and Vandel. They both appeared to be enjoying the moment. My admission that I had followed Torrance seemed to please them. They were like predators who had captured their prey.

"This is totally unfair. It's wrong to interrogate me again because of a simple misunderstanding. You can investigate me all you want — once a month, once a week, or every day — it doesn't matter. I've done nothing wrong."

Chapter 41: The Vote

ON NOVEMBER 4 my picture, along with three other city council candidates, was on the front page of the *Post Register*. It provided each of us an opportunity to answer common questions. My answers reflected my commitment to being a voice for everyone. I spoke about the need to consider all issues with the guiding principles of fairness, honesty, integrity, and compassion. After a long campaign the election was only two days away. Jasmine and Darius, along with other family and friends, had helped with the campaign.

With Election Day upon us, LaVonna and I were hopeful. On the night of the election we invited supporters to our home to watch the returns come in and celebrate with us. Unfortunately, things didn't go as planned. As the returns started coming in, it was clear this wasn't going to be a good night for me. Everyone expressed words of encouragement as they left. Most didn't wait for the final vote count. I smiled and thanked them, but the hurt was deeper than I had expected.

A few days after the election, one of the city council members announced he had been called to go on a Mormon mission and was resigning his seat on the council. According to the newspaper, the mayor indicated he would be selecting the interim replacement within the next few weeks. The mayor was quoted as saying he wanted to name someone who would contribute to making the city council more 'well rounded.'

Several friends told me they had contacted the mayor and recommended that he select me as the interim city councilman. LaVonna and I discussed whether it made sense for me to speak to the mayor. I was apprehensive to put my name in consideration because I didn't want to experience disappointment so soon after the election.

On November 11, 2007, I met with Mayor Fuhriman. I made my case that I was the right person at the right time to help lead the city. I emphasized my experience as the ethics officer for the laboratory. I explained how I could contribute to the decision making of the city leadership and emphasized the importance of ethics and transparency in government.

The mayor was polite and courteous in his response, but it was clear he had already made up his mind. He graciously shook my hand and said he would add my name to the list. I thanked him for his time and wished him well.

A few weeks later, it was announced that the mayor had made his selection. Yes, I was disappointed, but not disheartened. I had no regrets.

Chapter 42: Ridiculousness

On November 12 I was deposed by BEA's outside counsel, Larry Halvorson. As DeAnne and I entered the INL law library, the white-haired gentleman rose to greet us. He introduced himself and we took a seat opposite him.

Over the next few hours, Halvorson grilled me with questions. He asked about everything from where I lived to conversations from two years ago. I was troubled by a particular exchange. Halvorson was apparently trying to discredit my allegation that racial discrimination was a factor in the revocation of Loren's INL badge. The following exchange occurred:

Halvorson: "Had, in fact, Jodi indicated to you that she knew Loren was African American before she pulled his badge?"

Patterson: "No, she indicated she pulled up his picture before pulling it."

Halvorson: "Okay, and his picture would indicate that he was African American, correct?"

Patterson: "Yes."

Halvorson: "He's Black, I take it?"

Patterson: "I'm not following your question."

Halvorson: "His skin color is black?"

Patterson: "No."

Halvorson: "Oh, it's not?"

Patterson: "No."

Halvorson: "Loren isn't?"

Patterson: "No."

Halvorson: "Is he darker than you or lighter than you?"

Patterson: "Darker but not black."

Halvorson: "Okay, but you think that by looking at his picture, she would have known he was African American?"

Patterson: "Yes."

Halvorson: "I haven't seen his picture so I don't know."

Patterson: "When you said black, I presumed you meant color, and he's not black. He's African American."

Halvorson: "His skin color is dark; is that correct?"

Patterson: "Yes."

Halvorson seemed to suggest that Jodi Streier couldn't tell Loren was African American by looking at his picture. I didn't know if Jodi, Olsen, or someone else had come up with this line of defense, but it was beyond ridiculous.

Chapter 43: Round One

IN OCTOBER 2007 BEA had filed a summary judgment with the Hearing Officer, Adeyeye, with the intent of getting my original retaliation complaint (filed June 2006) dismissed. Because we hadn't heard anything by now, DeAnne and I presumed that the Hearing Officer wasn't going to grant the judgment.

On November 21, a week before the hearing, we received an official response from Adeyeye. Adeyeye ruled largely in favor of BEA. Adeyeye dismissed five of the six allegations cited in my original whistleblower complaint.

For two days, I mulled over the summary judgment. Finally, I realized that while I disagreed with Adeyeye's conclusions, they were consistent with DOE regulations. I was comforted by the fact that her decision was based on administrative requirements, not on the merits of my complaint.

DeAnne and I decided not to appeal. We believed that the retaliatory actions BEA took after I filed my whistleblower complaint were of greater significance and would be easier to prove. These actions included investigating me four times, disciplining me with time off without pay, and removing me from the Ethics Office.

LaVonna and I spent the weekend with family and friends. I spent most of Monday in DeAnne's office going over facts, dates, times, and places. The case file was well over a thousand pages with numerous citations and notations. The process would have been overwhelming except for the fact that I knew the information well. And I knew the truth didn't change with circumstances or time.

Chapter 44: Round Two

THE DOE HEARING began on Tuesday, November 27, 2007. I awoke with a sense of excitement. My day in court had finally arrived. As usual, I went outside to get the newspaper. The front-page headline read, "Doe Hearing Starts Today." I prepared my papers, put on my suit and tie, and was ready to go. LaVonna, Jasmine, and Darius were ready and waiting.

I had expected the hearing to be in one of the large courtrooms. When I opened the door, my jaw dropped. It was a small makeshift room with a table up front for the Hearing Officer and uncomfortable chairs for the attorneys, witnesses, and observers. As I approached the front of the room, I did a double take when I saw an African American female. Only after we greeted each other did I realize she had introduced herself as, "Valerie Adeyeye." It hit me; she was the Hearing Officer.

Growing up in Idaho Falls, I had never seen an African American judge, hearing officer, or any other official of the judicial system. It felt good knowing the case would be decided by an African American. DeAnne and I had speculated that BEA might try the 'angry black man' strategy in an effort to portray me in a negative light. If it was part of their strategy, I was sure they now had second thoughts. When Katherine Moriarty (BEA attorney) and Halvorson saw Adeyeye, they almost tripped over each other.

Adeyeye opened the hearing with a description of the DOE

hearing process and what to expect over the next four days. I was pleased to see reporters from local television stations and the *Post Register*. An investigator from the DOE Inspector General's Office was also present.

When one of the TV reporters prepared to set up her video camera, Adeyeye interrupted, "Cameras will not be allowed in the courtroom."

Adeyeye then asked everyone present to introduce themselves. Members of my family included my sisters, Norma Patterson, Judy Patterson, and Lou Swift; nephew Lee Swift (Angie); niece Nicole Swift with her daughters, Keisha and Mia; and my brother Don Patterson. My friend and pastor, Bob Sherwood, also attended.

Upon seeing so many of my family members present, Adeyeye commented, "You could have an early Thanksgiving right here."

DeAnne presented her opening statement: "Essentially the case we have today deals with Mr. Patterson and the actions he has taken to protect his own standards, his integrity, and the standards of BEA. I want to begin by giving you a quote from his most recent Performance Evaluation. This occurred on February 24 of 2006. Doug Benson, his immediate manager, in referring to Mr. Patterson, said, 'He knows and lives the standards without compromise.' And Mr. Benson is right. Mr. Patterson is willing to sacrifice his position, his chance of success, even his employment to protect BEA standards. But when he did so, he was subjected to retaliation. What he is not willing to sacrifice is his integrity, his personal standards, and BEA standards in the risks that their management caused."

Halvorson followed with his opening argument. I listened to him state that I had misused government equipment, failed to cooperate with Security's investigations, and was insubordinate by failing to disclose the confidential name.

At times, I could feel my blood pressure rise and my pulse quicken. It was hard to suppress the urge to interrupt when he said something that was untrue.

Following Halvorson's remarks, DeAnne called me to the stand and I was sworn in. DeAnne and I had previously agreed it would be best if I was the first person to testify. We believed it would be important for me to establish credibility with the hearing officer as soon as possible.

I took the witness chair, just a few feet from LaVonna and the kids. DeAnne had me review my personal history as well as my professional history at the laboratory. She had me read aloud excerpts from the past few years' performance appraisals. With pride and humility, I read the words that spoke about my outstanding performance and my commitment to setting the highest standards in ethical conduct.

DeAnne spent the rest of the day going over the facts and having me testify as to my actions and the actions of BEA management. By the end of the day, I was tired but feeling good. Day one had been a good day. We had established the foundation that BEA had indeed retaliated against me for filing the whistleblower complaint.

As we walked out of the hearing room, one of the waiting television reporters asked about the hearing.

"I believe we're off to a great start; justice will be served," I said.

That evening my family gathered around the dinner table and gave thanks. The Swifts visited for a couple of hours before driving back to Boise. We encouraged them to spend the night because it was beginning to snow and the roads would likely be dangerous. Unfortunately, they had to be at work the next morning. By the time they left it was close to ten o'clock. As I prepared for bed, I thanked LaVonna and the kids for all their love and support. I knew the next day would be the most challenging day for me. DeAnne had warned me that Halvorson's cross-examination would be grueling.

Chapter 45: Round Three

THE NEXT MORNING, as I prepared to leave, the phone rang. It was my sister Lou. She sounded exhausted. I asked her about the trip back to Boise.

"Well, you know, Buzz, we are lucky to be alive. We were about halfway home when we slid off the road; the SUV was on two wheels."

"Oh, my goodness."

"If not for the grace of God we wouldn't be here."

"I'm so glad everyone is okay. Love you, sis."

When LaVonna and I arrived at the courthouse, we were pleased to see my sister Norma already there and waiting for us. We gave her a hug and walked into the room. A few minutes later Adeyeye arrived and I was sworn in. Halvorson began his cross examination.

Halvorson spoke in a soft and deliberate manner. His presence was more comfortable than I expected.

"Dennis, do you believe you could effectively return to the position of ethics officer?"

"Yes, but only if Grossenbacher created the right work environment. He would have to set the standard by allowing employees to express their opinions."

Halvorson then attempted to make the case that BEA had an open-door policy and that I had always had free access to speak to Grossenbacher. I told Halvorson that BEA had no such policy and that when I told Olsen I wanted to meet with Grossenbacher, he responded with, "Do you really want to take me on?"

Halvorson spent considerable time cross examining me on my actions and statements on April 24, 2007. It was the meeting in which I refused to disclose the name of the confidential employee. He asked me several times whether in the past I had spoken to and challenged Benson as I had in this meeting. I shared previous examples where Benson and I had passionate discussions and strong disagreements. I told Halvorson I acted ethically and responsibly by honoring the employee's request that I not disclose the name to anyone.

"It was wrong for Benson and Middleton to try to force me to give up the name. For me to do so would be in violation of the INL Standards of Conduct and Business Ethics."

Halvorson questioned me about the August 2005 meeting with Juan Alvarez. Halvorson attempted to portray my conduct as inappropriate and unprofessional.

"All I did was express an opinion he didn't want to hear."

I noted that I informed Alvarez that his security managers had violated procedures and refused to cooperate with my investigation. I further testified, "I told Alvarez that I believed racial discrimination was a factor and if Loren had filed a complaint with the Idaho Human Rights Commission (IHRC) BEA would have lost." I reminded Halvorson that the very next day Alvarez issued a letter that basically described me as being unfit to be the ethics officer.

Halvorson then moved to the issue of whether I had violated company policy by writing and filing my whistleblower complaint on company time and equipment.

"This should never have been a question. A DOE contractor

employee indisputably has the right to file a DOE whistleblower complaint, and do so on company equipment and time."

The questioning then turned to the cell phone conversation I had with Security Investigator Torrance in September 2006 when he called while I was at the hospital with my friend AJ. This was the conversation where, according to Torrance, I refused to cooperate with him. I explained that when Torrance asked me if anyone had told me why I was being investigated I said I was choosing not answer at that time. I told Halvorson I was well within my rights not to answer that question and that it was unfair for BEA to later discipline me for this.

"AJ died the next day."

On redirect examination, DeAnne asked me about the Battelle Memorial Corporate investigative report dated December 2005. She read an excerpt from the report: "We recommend that BEA senior management evaluate and identify actions it considers appropriate to improve the working relationships between the Ethics Office and the involved managers and departments in this matter."

"Dennis, did BEA take any actions in response to this recommendation."

"No, they did nothing. If they had perhaps things might have turned out differently."

At noon, Halvorson concluded his cross-examination and we recessed for lunch.

Chapter 46: My Witnesses

THE AFTERNOON INCLUDED the testimony of friends and colleagues. I was confident their testimony would be powerful and convincing. All of them were well respected and highly regarded in the workplace and the community.

Our first witness was Bob Phipps, a manager who reported to Benson. I had often consulted with Bob on various issues. We had established a good working relationship based on trust and respect. Bob was the only current BEA employee I had requested to testify on my behalf. I knew that any employee who would dare to testify on my behalf would be risking his or her career to do so. I asked Bob because I believed he had the moral courage to tell the truth, even in the face of adversity.

After Bob reviewed his thirty-five years of laboratory experience, DeAnne asked him whether he had any prior experience with whistleblower complaints. Bob explained that in 2002 he was the manager of the legal function for Argonne National Laboratory West. He said that he had direct involvement with a prior DOE whistleblower. When asked, Bob told the court it was appropriate for me to have written my DOE whistleblower complaint using government time and equipment. Bob testified that he informed Benson and me of his opinion in 2006.

Bob testified that he was interviewed by Torrance and questioned about the allegation that I had been biased in my investigation of the Eric Greenwade matter.

Bob said, "I felt he (Dennis) tried very hard to stay in the middle of that issue, he was unbiased as much as he possibly could be, and was trying to get at the facts of the case."

When asked about his opinion of my character, Bob testified, "I believe he is a very honest individual who has strong beliefs in what is right and ethical, and that he sticks by those beliefs."

At the conclusion of Bob's testimony Adeyeye asked Bob his opinion as to whether Benson and I could work together again.

"I think they both would attempt to make the situation work." Halvorson's cross examination lasted only about ninety seconds and did nothing to discredit Bob's testimony.

The next witness called by DeAnne was Phil Wells. Phil had worked for Benson as an auditor from August 2000 through May 2003.

When asked about my character, Phil replied, "He was extremely professional. He was well known to always abide by any laws, rules, and professional ethics, whatever. It was known that he, if anything, went to the extreme to make sure everything was abided by."

DeAnne asked Phil about his experience with Benson.

"During my audits I was well known for being very detailed. There are things I began to uncover that I felt were unallowable, if not illegal, as far as reimbursement from the federal government. When I raised these objections, Mr. Benson did everything to quiet me, to make sure I did not bring them up. As I continued to bring them up, he became more irate."

DeAnne asked Phil if Benson ever did anything to keep him from raising issues.

"He made the point that I would have to send emails to him rather than directly to managers. He then would go in and change those emails to what he wanted to say, and forward it to the manager as though I had written them."

DeAnne asked Phil if he believed I could be reinstated to the position as ethics officer and be effective.

Phil responded, "Absolutely."

Halvorson's cross examination of Phil lasted less than two minutes and did nothing to detract from the credibility of his testimony. He noted that Phil sounded angry at Benson and asked if he was correct in his observation. Phil replied, "Yes, I feel he is a very dishonest individual."

After a brief recess, DeAnne called Katherine Moriarty, senior counsel for BEA. Moriarty was a witness for BEA, but DeAnne had determined that she could provide information useful to our side. Early in her testimony, Moriarty said she had been employed by BEA since February 2005. As she testified, it reminded me of something that DeAnne had shared with me shortly after I had contacted her to represent me. DeAnne told me that when BEA assumed the contract, Mark Olsen had offered her the job that Moriarty now held. Here we sat with BEA's first choice of legal counsel representing me and their second choice trying to defend BEA.

Moriarty confirmed that on September 6, 2006, she sent me an email admitting that it was appropriate for me to write my whistleblower complaint on my work computer and using work time. DeAnne also got Moriarty to admit that management, including senior BEA management, was aware I had filed the whistleblower complaint when they met to discuss the issues that led to my three-day suspension in October 2006. This demonstrated that BEA had a retaliatory motivation for their actions.

DeAnne grilled Moriarty on the fact that I was one of only eleven employees in the entire laboratory who received a zero-merit increase for the year 2006. This was a key element of my allegation that BEA had retaliated against me. Moriarty provided little explanation and hence had been a good witness for our side.

It was now time for the testimony of our star witness, John Denson. John held the position of president of the laboratory from October 1994 through September 1999 when the lab was managed by Lockheed Martin. During this time, I reported directly to John. We had a great working relationship.

A year ago, I had contacted John and told him of my situation.

"Is there anything I can do to help?" he had asked.

I paused before asking, "Would you be willing to fly out and testify on my behalf?"

"Yes, Dennis, I would be glad to testify about your character and integrity," he had responded.

DeAnne asked John to explain why the Ethics Office reported directly to him.

John replied, "It's the way Lockheed Martin's ethics program was set up. Each president was to have an ethics officer reporting directly to him but also with a dotted line responsibility to the corporation, which provided uniformity. And Dennis' job was to handle the ethics problems of our company and to report those to the corporation, and review those with me at least monthly."

DeAnne went on to ask John about my performance. John replied that I was a good performer and had received a couple of promotions.

DeAnne asked about the issue of confidentiality.

John replied, "I wanted everyone to feel they could go to the Ethics Office and not have anything happen to them. Their identity didn't have to be revealed to anyone other than the Ethics Office."

She asked if I ever had any conflict with senior management in the performance of my job. John replied yes, but noted that management knew he was going to support the Ethics Office.

John stated, "I don't think there's any way he could have done the job and not made some of these guys angry, because we had a big organization. There were six thousand people and there was always some conflict."

DeAnne asked about my interaction with management. John replied, "I never got anything but real good news about him out of our management team. They didn't always agree with him but they knew he was doing the job as well as he could. And so — I backed him on it."

DeAnne closed by asking John about my character.

John testified, "I wanted someone who would dig his heels in and do that job right, because it's the way Lockheed Martin operates. They want ethical conduct out of everybody. And since the president's responsible for everything, well, I had to have somebody I thought was of high character and good moral standing and ethical background. He satisfied all those things for me."

As I listened to the testimony of my former boss, I was humbled by his remarks. I was honored that he had taken the time to testify. To my knowledge, this was an unprecedented act. Never before in a DOE whistleblower case had a former president testified on behalf of the whistleblower. In my opinion, this spoke volumes about John's character and his commitment to doing the right thing.

Halvorson's cross examination lasted less than three minutes and did nothing to detract from the credibility of John's testimony.

The final witness called on my behalf was Joan Mehner. Joan was a good friend and had worked for me in the Ethics Office from 1997 through January 2005. Joan knew both Benson and me very well and could provide testimony about our individual character and integrity.

DeAnne asked Joan to describe me as a supervisor. Joan replied, "I would say he was probably one of the best managers I ever had in my whole career. I had one other who was outstanding and he is right up there with her."

Again, Halvorson's cross examination was brief and uneventful. Joan's testimony wrapped up things for the day. I left the courthouse feeling affirmed and more importantly blessed to have such positive people in my life, people of great courage and conviction.

Chapter 47: Day 3 — BEA Witnesses

THE THIRD DAY OF THE HEARING, Thursday, November 29, 2007, I awoke with great anticipation and a bit of trepidation. Today would be the testimony of my former boss, Doug Benson. Since 2005, I had come to see a side of Benson that others had told me about for years. The dishonesty, vengefulness, and self-serving nature of Benson's personality had come front and center. Today was my opportunity to see firsthand how he would answer questions under oath, with the potential penalty of imprisonment.

Benson approached the bench with a swagger. He glanced over at me. He raised his right hand and swore to tell the truth. Benson was asked about his responsibilities as the director of Internal Audit and Ethics. He stated that his organization was responsible for conducting independent reviews on behalf of management to ensure that management objectives were being met, that they were in compliance with laws, regulations, contract, and DOE Orders. He said he was also responsible for the Ethics Office.

Benson spent the next two hours describing my alleged misconduct and justifying his disciplinary actions against me.

When asked about the possibility of me being reinstated to the Ethics Office he responded, "I don't see how that could — I don't see how that could function." I was not surprised by his testimony; it just reinforced the fact that BEA would do everything possible to make sure I would never again be the ethics officer for the INL.

Under cross-examination DeAnne asked Benson, "When you first met Mr. Patterson, what was your impression?"

Benson replied, "He was very professional."

"And you would agree that he was well respected as the ethics officer, correct?"

Benson replied, "Yes."

DeAnne continued, "And I think you already testified, too, and you won't dispute that you evaluated Mr. Patterson as Outstanding in the years prior to the 2006 evaluation, correct?"

"That's correct," Benson testified.

DeAnne asked Benson about the investigative report authored by the Battelle Corporate Office in early 2006. DeAnne read from the report: "We recommend that BEA senior management evaluate and identify actions it considers appropriate to improve the working relationship between the Ethics Office and the involved managers and departments in this matter."

DeAnne continued, "Isn't it true that BEA senior management did not take any action with regard to that recommended action from Corporate?'

"Formal action? No, they did not," Benson said.

Deanne asked further, "So, is it true that senior management didn't take any specific action as was recommended in the Corporate Report?"

Benson replied, "I didn't see individuals who this was addressed to take an action, no."

As I listened to this testimony it angered me to hear what I already knew. No one, including Olsen, Middleton, Alvarez, Grossenbacher, gave a rat's behind about me. It was egregious for BEA to totally ignore a recommendation from Battelle corporate. Their failure to do so didn't harm anyone except me. I remembered the words of a supposed BEA guiding principle: "respect and caring for our people." I had been treated as less than a person, as disposable and without value.

In further addressing the corporate report, DeAnne asked Benson, "And would you agree with me that the report also indicates Mr. Patterson is, indeed, a very skilled investigator?"

Benson replied, "Yes, it does say that."

DeAnne asked Benson about Olsen's opinion that it was inappropriate for me to write my whistleblower complaint on company time and equipment. Benson acknowledged that Olsen's opinion was wrong and that had I not fought this issue it would have posed a risk to BEA in future whistleblower actions. Benson also acknowledged that my actions led to policy changes that protected the rights of employees.

Halvorson asked Benson about my removal from the ethics position. "Was Mr. Patterson's refusal to disclose the name of the sources a factor in his directed reassignment?"

Benson: "Not in my opinion; no."

In my opinion, Benson had just lied under oath. I conferred with DeAnne.

Halvorson concluded his examination. DeAnne began her cross examination. She handed Benson the letter authored and signed by him June 13, 2007.

DeAnne: "If you will take a look at that document, second paragraph: Isn't it true that you specifically identify one of the actions that caused the directed reassignment was Mr. Patterson's failure to provide the name?"

Benson: "That's how this reads, yes."

DeAnne: "No further questions."

Halvorson: "Nothing further."

Benson's testimony was directly contradicted by a letter authored and signed by him. I wondered whether or not Adeyeye would take punitive action against Benson. I was almost certain that BEA wouldn't take any action for his not telling the truth under oath.

The next to testify was the Security investigator. Torrance testified that Katherine Moriarty asked him to investigate me for misuse of government equipment in June 2006. He further testified it was Moriarty who asked him to investigate me a second time in August 2006 for alleged bias involving Eric Greenwade.

Torrance said that he had never before investigated anyone for bias and that it was not something Security would normally investigate.

Torrance testified that he filed a complaint against me on September 21, 2006. Torrance said he saw me walking behind him and assumed my intent was to intimidate him. He testified that he contacted Zabala and reported me. Torrance provided no other testimony to support his allegation that I had intended to intimidate him.

My new boss, Ed Anderson, was called to the stand by Halvorson as a BEA witness. However, his testimony turned out to be more helpful to me. He testified that in our first meeting I raised questions about my qualifications for the job.

"Dennis was very clear that he was — he made the statement that he's going to be as good as he can be, whatever we've got for him to do. And he's done that. It's been comfortable, not combative at all." Ed also testified that prior to my being assigned to his division he had never seen my resume.

Toni Vandel was called as a witness for BEA. She discussed her and Zabala's interrogation of me on May 16, 2007, in response to Middleton and Benson accusing me of improper conduct when they directed me on April 24 to disclose the confidential name.

When asked about my demeanor in the interview she replied, "He was very business-like, serious. He was not hostile; he was just there to answer the questions."

Vandel was asked about the disciplinary action meeting where it was decided I would be transferred to engineering. Vandel said Zabala stated that I did not deny Middleton and Benson's allegations that I had treated them with disrespect. She said based on this information they decided to remove me from the Ethics Office. Those who participated in the disciplinary decision included Benson, Zabala, Mark Holubar (HR director), Mark Olsen, and Art Clark.

When Zabala testified about my conduct in the same May 16 meeting, she testified under oath, "He (Dennis Patterson) was hostile and very condescending, and it was difficult to talk with him."

So, while Vandel described me as business-like, now I was being described as hostile. Zabala testified that in the discipline meeting three options were discussed: termination, suspension, and reassignment.

During testimony Zabala acknowledged that the company did not have a written open-door policy.

DeAnne asked Zabala about my alleged inappropriate statements made to Benson and Middleton. Zabala had stated that I admitted making the statements. However, under cross-examination she admitted that she never asked me if I admitted or denied making the statements.

DeAnne: "You'll agree that you never asked him to confirm or deny whether he made those statements?"

Zabala: "No, I told him those were the statements attributed to him in that meeting."

Earlier, when cross-examining Vandel, DeAnne questioned her about BEA's attempt to equate my alleged misconduct and discipline to another event. DeAnne got Vandel to admit that one of the so-called 'similar events' involved serious misconduct by Security officers.

In her testimony Vandel said, "The horseplay involved the

Security Department and some individuals. You would liken it to something like hazing, like an initiation; individuals had been tied up, and then photographs taken with the guards." She testified it didn't include nudity. I smiled as I listened, because I had heard from several credible sources that this incident involved nudity, duct tape, and a gun.

Vandel failed in her attempt to equate my situation to this egregious act of misconduct by employees responsible for protecting the property and people of the INL. There were two obvious differences between these security individuals and me. One, they were white, and two they had not filed complaints against BEA senior managers. In my opinion, this was an example of white privilege and how things were at the INL.

The next BEA witness was Dyanna. Her testimony was important because she was the Security investigator who insisted I disclose the confidential source. Under cross-examination she noted that at the time the issue came up she had only been employed at the INL for seventeen days. Specific to the issue of confidentiality, the following questions and answers occurred between DeAnne and Dyanna:

DeAnne: "Well, isn't it true that you had received an email from not only Mr. Patterson, but Mr. Benson —"

Dyanna: "Um-hum"

DeAnne: "— saying that confidentiality could not be breached."

Dyanna: "I did receive those emails, yes."

DeAnne: "And still, based on that direction from his up-line management, you still believed that Mr. Patterson was failing to cooperate with your investigation?"

Dyanna: "I still believe to this day that Mr. Patterson failed to cooperate with my investigation."

DeAnne: "And do you have any support from your supervisors toward that opinion?"

Dyanna: "My supervisor … Mr. Middleton."

It was now turn for my former friend and neighbor, Security Director Tom Middleton, to testify. By now, I had come to expect the worst from Middleton and so I thought nothing was going to surprise me. I was wrong!

Middleton was asked about whether he supported Dyanna's insistence that I disclose the name of the confidential source. Middleton said he did and that was the reason he was in the April 16, 2007, meeting with Benson and me.

DeAnne got Middleton to admit that Dyanna had interviewed the confidential source telephonically prior to April 16, 2007, and that I had arranged for that anonymous phone call. Nonetheless, Middleton was absolute in asserting that there was no other option than for me to disclose the confidential name and that my failure to do so was unacceptable. He went on to describe me in the harshest of terms.

Halvorson: "Do you believe you could work effectively with Patterson if he were reinstated to the position of ethics officer?

Middleton: "I would have to say I cannot. The other grave concern is Dennis rejected his manager's authority over him … an investigator who has come to the conclusion that he's above the law, that he has no authority over him is a person who is going to hurt people unnecessarily … the license to investigate without management oversight is where you get the Gestapo."

There was an audible gasp from the courtroom when Middleton used the word Gestapo.

DeAnne, in cross-examination, read from my email: "I am willing to contact the employee and ask her if she would be willing to sit down with Dyanna and/or call Dyanna a second time …

anonymously and visit with her."

DeAnne asked Middleton why this wasn't an acceptable option versus forcing me to disclose the confidential name.

Middleton replied, "With that proposal the problem is I don't know what the source said. I don't know what the source has actually said."

Middleton provided no credible explanation for why he and Benson had tried to force me to disclose a confidential source.

DeAnne read for Middleton an email that Benson wrote when Security initially requested the identity of the confidential source, "Confidentiality is required by the Employee Concern Order, as with my other investigative process. We cannot breach that requirement. The employee must make their decision."

Middleton testified that he only learned of this email from Benson a few days ago, but that it didn't change his opinion.

During Middleton's direct examination he stated that he felt threatened by some of our interactions such as my not speaking to him in the hall, supposedly staring at him from across the street, and allegedly cutting him off as we left our driveways. Appallingly, he said that he was concerned for the safety of his family. Under cross-examination the following exchange occurred:

DeAnne: "And you asserted that you had to question whether this might be a risk for your family, is that right?"

Middleton: "I felt like my family — I was worried that my family was at risk. I didn't know."

DeAnne: "Well, isn't it true that your daughter and Mr. Patterson's daughter are friends?"

Middleton: "Yes, they go to school together and have been friends for ten years."

DeAnne: "And isn't it true that after that time, you still allowed your daughter to go over to his home?"

Middleton: "I did."

DeAnne: "Even though you had this fear?"

Middleton: "I allowed them to go to school together, too; yeah."

In one breath he said he was afraid I might harm his family and in the next he admitted to allowing his daughter to come over to our home unsupervised. I looked at the hearing officer as Middleton testified on this subject. Even she seemed to be taken aback by his testimony.

Katherine Moriarty was called to the stand by Halvorson. Moriarty testified that she was the person who requested that I be investigated for misuse of property in June 2006. She noted that she had earlier advised me about a "prohibition against using government time to pursue personal matters."

She further testified, "When the Idaho Human Rights Commission contacted me and told me that Mr. Patterson was asking to withdraw his complaint, I asked the IHRC investigator for more details. She indicated, 'Well I can send you those. He (Dennis) sent those (emails) to me from his government computer. I'll just forward those to you.' And so, when I received those emails I looked at them and was very surprised, because I understood that Patterson had agreed with me that he was not going to use government time or equipment to pursue this personal claim … it was at that point I decided an investigation was necessary."

This testimony illustrated some of the craziness that had occurred. Moriarty testified that she had me investigated for misuse of government equipment even though she knew the reason I sent the emails was to request dismissal of my discrimination complaint. This confirmed, in my mind, that the real reason she had me investigated was because she had learned I had filed my whistleblower complaint.

Under questioning by DeAnne, Moriarty acknowledged that

shortly after April 15, 2007, she pulled my emails and thereby identified the name of the confidential employee. Thus Benson, Middleton, and Olsen had the name of the employee prior to authoring the letter demanding that I release the name. It was all just a ruse to get me out of the Ethics Office.

Chapter 48: The Close

FRIDAY, THE LAST DAY OF THE HEARING, I was looking forward to DeAnne's closing argument. In the trial scenes I had seen on TV, the closing arguments always made for great drama. Unfortunately, it was late in the day when testimony from BEA's witnesses concluded. DeAnne and Halvorson agreed to forego the closing arguments with the stipulation that they would file closing briefs at a later date.

At 4:53 p.m. Adeyeye adjourned the hearing. I put my arm around LaVonna and held her close. I remembered Proverbs 10: 9: "A man of integrity walks securely, but he who takes a crooked path will be found out." My integrity had withstood the attacks from BEA and the crooked ways of BEA had been found out. God had answered our prayers.

DeAnne and Halvorson shook hands like two fighters at the end of a championship match. Halvorson whispered to DeAnne, "Excellent job of finding all our weaknesses." Obviously, DeAnne had performed exceptionally well. We made an awesome team.

I shook hands with Adeyeye and said, "Thanks for what you do. I hope you enjoyed your time in Idaho Falls."

"Well, it was quite an experience. I've never been part of a hearing with so much media coverage," she replied.

As Adeyeye prepared to leave the room I overheard a reporter ask when a decision would be rendered.

"In approximately thirty to sixty days," she said. This meant we would have an answer by the end of January, 2008. I was happy to know this would all be over soon.

***

Prior to the hearing I was hopeful that a potentially very important witness would testify on my behalf. This person had been the DOE–Idaho Employee Concerns Program Manager from approximately 2000 through the middle of 2005. His role and responsibility had included oversight of the BEA Ethics Office. Over the years we had developed a strong professional relationship. His name was Paul Allen. Like his father, Tony Allen, who was my friend and mentor, Paul was a person of honor and integrity.

In August 2007, I asked him to meet me in the company cafeteria. We had a cup of coffee and I updated him on the status of my whistleblower case. Paul expressed confidence in the DOE process as well as his respect for me. After several minutes, I mustered the courage to ask, "Would you be willing to testify at the hearing as a character witness?"

"I would be glad to. I don't see a problem; DOE doesn't have a dog in the fight." He paused, then added, "Well, maybe I better check with legal before I commit."

"Thanks, this really means a lot to me. Please get back to me as soon as possible," I said.

I didn't hear back from Paul, so I decided to send him an email. In his response, he informed me that after speaking to DOE–ID legal he determined that DOE–ID did indeed "have a dog in the fight. I better not testify on your behalf because it might seem as though I would be taking a position contrary to DOE." I suspected that by 'legal,' he meant Eva Auman. She was the attorney who had sided with Olsen and had said it was wrong of me to write my whistleblower complaint on my work computer. DOE–ID should have been an advocate for whistleblowers, not working hand in glove with BEA.

***

The other missing witness was Knut Meyerin. In 2006, Knut had informed the *Post Register* about my whistleblower against BEA. He had also offered to attend the hearing as an advocate. Knut was the regional representative for Idaho Senator Larry Craig. Unfortunately, during the interim Knut had resigned because of a national scandal related to Craig. In my opinion, Knut did the right and honorable thing by resigning, but it would have been advantageous for me if he hadn't.

Chapter 49: We Should Not Be Deterred

I WAS LOOKING FORWARD to the 2008 Dr. King banquet. Anthony Hebron was our keynote speaker. Hebron was a corporate executive vice president for Battelle Memorial Institute. He was flying to Idaho Falls on a Battelle corporate jet and I would be meeting him at the Aeromark airport. As I waited in the lobby, I wondered if Hebron had any knowledge of my whistleblower complaint. It was likely that someone from BEA had told him about it. As I gazed out the window, I saw the jet land and begin coasting up to the small airport lobby. I watched as it slowly taxied to a stop. The steps to the jet slowly deployed.

The first person who stepped off the plane was Anthony. He was readily recognizable. It wasn't often an African American departed from a corporate jet in Idaho Falls. As he reached the bottom of the steps, I saw another person exit the plane. It was Grossenbacher.

In December I had asked Grossenbacher, via email, to say a few words at the MLK banquet. He initially accepted. Then, with no explanation, his office contacted me and told me he wouldn't be able to attend. Now, here he was walking toward the airport lobby with Anthony. I expected Grossenbacher to enter with Hebron and do the introductions.

Fifteen feet from the door, Grossenbacher took a left turn and disappeared. I couldn't believe it. Sitting together on the small jet, surely Anthony told him I was waiting for him. Yet Grossenbacher chose to leave without even a hello. I walked to the entrance and welcomed Anthony.

As we drove to the hotel, Anthony asked me what it was like to be African American and live in Idaho Falls. I told him it was a great place to raise a family. I told Anthony about a racial discrimination incident that had occurred at the INL several years ago.

After listening, he remarked, "Dennis, it is sad that such things continue to happen in today's world."

I was tempted to tell him I was a whistleblower and that discrimination was part of the story, but I didn't want to get him involved.

When Anthony and I entered the banquet room I was pleased to see the room filled to capacity. Anthony and I took our seats at the head table. Seated to my left was Anthony and to his left, Beth Sellers, Manager of DOE Idaho. This was mind-blowing — a whistleblower, an executive from the company's corporate office, and the head of DOE – Idaho having a meal together.

Unbeknownst to anyone but a handful of us, there was another bizarre situation in the room. Mayor Fuhriman was seated at a table to my right. He was at the table with the members of his newly formed Race Relations Committee. The mayor had created the committee to improve race relations in Idaho Falls.

The committee's vice-chair was Isaac Simmons, director of BEA's Protective Force Security division. I had learned from a friend in Human Resources that Isaac had been suspended without pay by Middleton for allegedly pointing a gun at a colleague's head and threatening to kill him. Isaac had called me during the Christmas holidays and told me his version. He said there was a gun involved but he never pointed it at anyone. It was just horseplay. He explained that he and the colleague were good friends and it happened at the person's home, not on company property. Isaac said no one, including Middleton, thought it was serious enough to report the incident to the police. As a result, Isaac said he was hopeful he wouldn't be terminated.

This incident was very similar to one that occurred in January 1995. In that case the laboratory's General Counsel (same position as Mark Olsen) Steve Brumley was arrested for pointing a gun at an INL colleague at the apartment complex where they lived. The arrest was front page news on January 18, 1995. To my knowledge the attorney was never disciplined. Instead, a few months later he was transferred to another facility. The main difference in these two cases was that Isaac was African American and the attorney was white. I learned later that Isaac was terminated by Middleton. To me, this was another example of white privilege.

Anthony began his keynote address: "Dr. King was an extraordinary man and a humble man. The night before he was gunned down, he asked people to remember him not for his honors or awards, but for how he helped his fellow man. Dr. King was a man of great faith. Operating in that faith he left a challenge for us and that challenge is to abandon the comfort of complacency."

Anthony went on to discuss the importance of diversity in the highest echelons of agencies and organizations. He challenged individuals to "do the best job you can," and organizations to take actions that result in measurable progress. He concluded his speech with, "We still have a lot of work ahead, and we've got some risks we all have to take. But we must remember that back in the 60s that vision of nightsticks, demon dogs, and Sheriff Bull Connor's minions attacking civil rights workers, those were Dr. King's followers. Those actions did not deter them and we should not be deterred now."

At the end of the evening, while shaking Anthony's hand, I said, "I was inspired and encouraged by your talk tonight. One day I will be able to tell you why." One day I would tell him about my not being deterred by racism, hatred, and vindictiveness — actions perpetrated by BEA senior management, some of whom were present and sitting at a table only a few feet from where he was speaking.

Chapter 50: Yes, We Can

SENATOR BARACK OBAMA had just won the Iowa Primary. It seemed that America was open to electing its first African American president. I was telling family, friends, and colleagues that Obama was the best person to lead our country. Of course, making such statements in one of the reddest, whitest, most conservative states in the nation was rarely received with enthusiasm. Nonetheless, I was a believer.

When LaVonna and I heard that Obama was going to be in Boise on Saturday, February 2, there was no way we would miss seeing him. We heard on the news that more than 10,000 were expected. Half-jokingly, I told LaVonna I was going to shake his hand. We arrived in Boise the night before and stayed with my sister Lou.

The next morning the family was up early. We arrived at the Taco Bell Arena before 6 a.m. There were already hundreds of people in line. It did my heart good to see such an incredible turnout for an African American Democrat in Idaho. The atmosphere in the arena was like being at a rock concert.

Obama walked onto the raised platform. Music played loud and the sense of anticipation was palpable. Obama smiled and waved to the crowd.

"And they told me there weren't any Democrats in Idaho, but

I did not believe them, I did not believe them." The roar of approval was deafening.

Obama said his hope for the future of America was an important part of his message. He said that people were beginning to call him a 'hope monger.' The crowd erupted with laughter. I listened intently to his dream of a better America. His message of "Yes we can," and an America that was inclusive instead of exclusive was invigorating.

Obama ended with, "This is our moment, this is our time . . . We will remake this country and together we will remake the world." I was energized, empowered, and encouraged.

As he ended his speech, LaVonna said, "Why don't you go down and see if you can shake his hand." Without pause, I gave her a peck on the cheek and ran down the steps.

As I approached the stadium floor, I couldn't see Obama. Then I spotted a boom microphone moving along in front of the crowd. Keeping an eye on the microphone, I moved people aside, gently most of the time. Finally, I saw him. He was shaking hands with anyone who got their hand close to him. When I got just to the right of him, I stood on my tiptoes and reached my hand over the outstretched hands of several others.

As he passed in front of me, I yelled, "Barack." Our eyes met for a fleeting moment. He reached out and shook my hand. It was a firm handshake, one I wouldn't soon forget.

I couldn't believe my good fortune. Of the more than fourteen thousand people at the rally I was one of the lucky ones. I was thrilled and honored. I couldn't wait to get back to Lavonna and tell her that I shook the hand of our future president.

The smile on LaVonna's face told me she already knew. She saw me shake his hand.

As we made our way to the exit a young lady ran up behind us and grabbed the sleeve of my coat. "Hey, I think I saw you shake Obama's hand."

"Yep, I did," I said.

"Can I shake your hand? I want to tell my friends, I shook the hand of the man who shook Obama's."

I gave her a firm handshake and a smile.

What a great ending to a great experience. LaVonna commented that the only thing she regretted was that she was so excited she forgot to take a picture. I told her it didn't matter because I had the memory of the moment. Our family and friends would just have to believe us when we told the story.

The next day my sister Lou called and told me that my picture, reaching out to shake Obama's hand was in the Boise paper, the *Idaho Statesman*. I would always cherish my picture with our future president.

Chapter 51: Keeping the Faith

HEARING OFFICER ADEYEYE did not render the decision within the projected thirty to sixty days. For all I knew, the decision could be made today, tomorrow, or months from now. DOE had the power to grant itself extension after extension without any recourse. All I could do was wait.

In late February, I heard that BEA was in the process of hiring a new ethics and employee concerns program manager. She was from the Hanford, Washington area and was moving to Idaho Falls in March. I believed that BEA was hiring her at this time to strengthen their case for not reinstating me in the position. BEA had argued at the hearing that I should not be reinstated. By filling the position before DOE–OHA issued the decision, they could also argue it would create a hardship on the newly-hired employee.

In early March, I walked by my old office and saw someone sitting at the desk. Over the next several weeks, I was in communication with my friends in the Internal Audit division. They told me the new person was not happy in her job. They said she felt like BEA had misrepresented the job and job duties. She was only with BEA a few months. One day she walked in, submitted her resignation to Benson, and left the same day. I had little doubt that BEA had once again walked down a crooked path. It appeared Benson had once again not been truthful.

With increasing regularity, I had to take a few hours of personal leave to make it through the week. The stress of waiting for the decision from DOE and the worry of what else could go wrong was getting unbearable.

In the spring of 2008 LaVonna and I joined a prayer and study group at our church. We met weekly to study scripture, pray, and encourage each other.

***

Prayer is a powerful thing. And it's a good thing. In the midst of my traumatic experience with INL, LaVonna's workplace was also experiencing trauma and was also front-page news. LaVonna had been working at Family Care Center (FCC) for the past few years as the director of Counseling Services. She had shared with me the ongoing turmoil between the FCC executive director, Dr. Thana Singarajah, and the board of FCC. It all came tumbling out in public on May 18. The *Post Register* reported that on April 28, Dr. Thana, at the request of the board, had been escorted from the FCC building by two Idaho Falls police officers. The board had alleged financial irregularities against Dr. Thana. And in turn, Dr. Thana had accused the FCC Board Chairman of lying.

During the next couple of months LaVonna and I discussed what was in her best interest given the happenings with FCC. She shared her desire to start her own business as a counselor and licensed psychologist. After much prayer and reflection, she decided to take a leap of faith. She resigned her position with Family Care and launched her own business: Dr. LaVonna Patterson, Patterson Compassionate Counseling. The business name reflected her passion for people and her desire to help with care and understanding. I was immensely proud of her.

LaVonna had come from humble beginnings, but had a life full of blessings. She had become a Christ follower at fourteen. Her faith strengthened my faith.

Chapter 52: Breathless

THE DOE OFFICE of Hearings and Appeals had announced that the decision would be issued in April. Though disappointed by the delay, I was excited about the timing because my birthday was April 14. As soon as I woke up on the 14th I checked my email and text for the good news. Unfortunately, my birthday came and went without any word from the hearing officer. Each subsequent week began with hope and ended in despair.

On June 13, I sat in my cubicle and reflected upon my work life. Exactly a year ago, I had been involuntarily transferred to my current position in engineering. It had been a difficult time, but I had performed well and received a good performance appraisal. I was thankful that my new management had treated me well and given me the chance to succeed. However, the job was still a very poor match for my skills and abilities. My passion was helping employees, not pretending to be an engineer. Waiting day by day for the hearing officer's decision, working in such conditions was taking its toll on me. There were days when I felt out of breath, anxious, worried, and at times, depressed. But through it all, I knew I was blessed with the love of family and the support of friends.

June 20, 2008, was a beautiful day with white fluffy clouds scudding across a deep blue sky. LaVonna and I had to drive to Boise to pick up Jasmine, who had spent the prior few days at a church camp a hundred miles north of Boise. We had been on the interstate for only about twenty minutes when my cell phone rang. I looked at the caller ID.

"Sweetheart, it's DeAnne; I think this is it."

"Hello," I answered breathlessly.

"Dennis, we just received the decision from Adeyeye. We won!" she proclaimed.

"LaVonna, we won!" I reached over and grabbed her hand.

My heart felt like it was going to burst and I was grinning ear to ear.

I pulled into a rest area. DeAnne continued, "The report found that BEA retaliated against you on five separate occasions, concluding with removing you from the position of ethics officer."

"DeAnne, thank you; this feels so good," I replied.

I jumped out of the car and ran around to the other side. I grabbed LaVonna in my arms, lifted her off the ground, and yelled, "God is so good, sweetheart."

As I looked around, I could see people looking at us, probably wondering what was going on and why we were celebrating in the parking lot of a rest area. We held hands as we walked around the grassy area of the rest stop. It felt so good being together when we received the news. There is nothing like having the person you love share in the joys of life.

As we left the rest area, I remembered that I had told Sven Berg, the reporter for the *Post Register*, that I would call him when I received the decision. I called and told him the results.

He asked for my thoughts on the outcome. I said, "I was confident from day one. I believed that the hearing officer would make the right decision and this would be to the benefit of many people besides myself."

Sven said the story would appear in the newspaper the following morning. I was pleased that the information would be published so quickly. It was important for the Idaho Falls community and even the rest of the country to know what had happened. Perhaps the news could be a ray of hope for other employees and a deterrent to companies.

As we continued the drive, the green fields seemed to be greener, the blue sky bluer, and the white clouds whiter. When we arrived at the Nazarene Church, I could see Jasmine anxiously waiting for us. It was good to see her pretty smiling face after being away for several days. I decided to wait until we got home to tell her the good news. It was great to listen to her excitedly tell about the happenings at church camp. The stories left no doubt that it had been a fun and rewarding experience.

Upon arriving home, we shared the good news with Jasmine and Darius. We had a big family hug and the kids told me how proud they were of me. For the first time in a long time, it felt like all was well.

Later that evening I logged onto my computer so I could read the entirety of the DOE–OHA decision. As DeAnne had explained, the letter contained the following:

- The security investigation of me for 'bias' was retaliation.
- The three-day suspension in October 2006 was retaliation.
- The low performance appraisal dated January 10, 2007, was retaliation.
- The zero-merit increase for 2006 was retaliation.
- Removing me from the ethics position was retaliation.

The decision directed BEA to do the following:

- Remove suspension notice and poor performance appraisal from my personnel file.
- Provide a retroactive merit increase for 2006.
- Reimburse lost pay for participating in the hearing proceedings.
- Reimbursement for attorney fees.

- Within thirty days of decision, BEA shall notify Patterson if there is a vacancy comparable to Patterson's previous position.

Unfortunately, the hearing officer did not require BEA to reinstate me as ethics officer. The decision cited the fact that the position had been modified and had been lowered from a specialist 5 to a 4 or 3. The decision stated, "As senior/auditor/employee concerns manager under Benson's new position, Patterson would be subject to an even lower salary scale and would be effectively demoted."

The report contained the following notation, "However, if Patterson so chooses, he should be considered for rotation into this position, especially in light of BEA's expressed desire to salvage his career at INL."

Note 19 of the report stated, "Some of the complaints against Patterson's behavior seem exaggerated. There is no evidence in the record of aggressive, threatening behavior by Patterson."

The report also contained the following notation regarding the Summary Judgment granted to BEA on November 21, 2007: "As noted in Section I.B., I dismissed this complaint on procedural grounds. Nonetheless, it appears, based on the findings of the ROI, that there was substantive merit to the disclosures, which alleged an abuse of authority related to violations of company procedure. The focus of this Decision is not, however, on the allegations contained in the first complaint but on those alleged retaliatory actions that occurred after Patterson filed his first (whistleblower) complaint, as the mere filing of this complaint constituted protected conduct under Part 708."

This was a direct reference to the actions of BEA in the Loren Mitchell matter in 2005. It was affirming and vindicating to read that there was substantive merit regarding my allegation of abuse of authority by BEA management.

As midnight approached, I couldn't sleep. The excitement of the day was still with me and my thoughts continued to race. I decided to send an email to all my friends and supporters to let them know the good news. I went into my office, just down from our master bedroom, and prepared the message. I told everyone of DOE's decision and thanked them for their support. The email went out to close to a hundred individuals across the country, from California to North Carolina.

The next morning, I awoke early. I walked out to get the newspaper. As I picked up the paper, I looked at the front page. The headline: "Doe Finds in Favor of INL Employee."

Chapter 53:
"Justice Delayed is Justice Denied"

NOT SURPRISINGLY, BEA continued its pattern of abuse. Instead of admitting wrongdoing, three days later, INL Communications Department issued the following iNote: "We believe that we acted appropriately and fairly in the case of Mr. Patterson when he filed three complaints against the company between June and October 2006. A decision concerning a possible appeal from the ruling is pending."

According to the DOE letter, BEA had fifteen days to decide.

On day thirteen, July 3, 2008 LaVonna, Jasmine, and I flew to Myrtle Beach, South Carolina to spend the holiday with LaVonna's family. On Independence Day we had a big barbeque and watched the fireworks on the beach. The next couple of days were relaxing, but I knew things could change in the blink of an eye.

On the morning of July 7 I awoke early and took a walk around the resort. I stopped by the small café, got a cup of coffee, and returned to our room. I joined LaVonna out on the balcony. We talked about the great time we were having. Just then my cell phone rang.

"It's DeAnne," I told LaVonna.

"Hello, Dennis," DeAnne said. I could tell by the sound of her voice that it wasn't good news. She continued, "BEA is appealing

DOE's decision."

After finishing the call, I held LaVonna's hand. "It's not over," I told her.

I explained the appeal process and what it meant to our future. I told her that it could be several months before DOE would make a determination.

I barely had time to digest the news when I received a call from the reporter, Sven Berg. He wanted my response to the appeal.

"I am fully confident that Adeyeye's ruling will be upheld. BEA can't change the facts."

Despite the bad news, I was determined that nothing would keep us from enjoying our vacation. I focused on the goodness of life instead of the hardship ahead.

When I returned to work it was weird knowing everything that had transpired while I was away in Myrtle Beach. The *Post Register* had run a front-page story with the headline, "Appeal is Filed in Whistle-Blower Case."

Additionally, BEA issued an iNote to all employees on July 8, 2008. The iNote was issued by Mark Olsen with 'concurrence' from Grossenbacher. I could only imagine the story Olsen must have told to convince Admiral Grossenbacher that it was a good idea to appeal. I wondered if Grossenbacher read the report or if he just took the word of Olsen that BEA had treated me fairly.

The iNote said in part: "We have chosen to appeal the decision because, among other reasons, we believe that (I) the hearing officer's findings of fact and conclusions of law, in several instances, are conflicting, and (II) the conclusions of retaliation are against the weight of the evidence presented at the hearing ... litigation is a lousy way to resolve disputes; but, when litigation occurs, we prefer to try the case in the court having jurisdiction over the particular case, rather than trying the case in the 'court of public opinion' or the media. However, when the media becomes heavily involved, we are going to respond appropriately to make clear why we have selected the particular course of action in question."

I was surprised at the tone of the iNote. In my opinion there was a not-so-subtle message: any employee who files a whistleblower complaint against the company will be fought to the very end. I provided a copy to DeAnne. She too was disturbed by the iNote and commented that the note itself appeared to be an act of retaliation.

***

On July 17, 2008, I received a copy of BEA's appeal letter to DOE–OHA. DeAnne and I had speculated on what grounds they might appeal and what specific issues they would contest. We figured they might challenge a few of the more substantive decisions of the hearing officer. As it turned out, BEA used classic big corporate strategy; concede nothing and contest everything. The 148-page appeal letter stated that the hearing officer 'erred' on sixty different occasions. DeAnne and I believed this was an abuse of the DOE process. Responding to such a lengthy brief was going to be exhaustive, costly, and would substantially delay the appeal decision. If the purpose was to wear me down, it wasn't going to work. DeAnne and I put together a response that we believed would shine a light on the abusive practices of BEA.

On August 8, BEA sent out the following iNote announcement: "Doug Benson, INL Director of Audits, will begin a six-month professional development opportunity at Battelle Memorial Institute in Columbus, Ohio, effective mid-September. Upon completion of the assignment at Battelle Columbus, Doug will have the opportunity to return to INL or assume a position with BMI or another of its affiliates."

DOE had found Benson guilty of retaliation; he had lied under oath, and instead of being disciplined, he got an assignment at corporate with all the perks. This was white privilege personified.

Those with the power and authority are treated differently than others. At the INL those in power did not include African Americans.

On October 6, 2008, employees received a special announcement. The iNote read, "DOE Special Assessment: BEA to retain INL contract to 2014." My stomach churned as I read DOE–ID manager, Beth Seller's statement: "I'm very encouraged by the performance of BEA, its management, and you — the employees — in these key transitional years of the laboratory." The iNote included Grossenbacher's response, "To me, the message is that we are here to stay."

The thought that BEA 'was here to stay' made me almost throw up. I had been through so much already. But aside from my personal trauma, I was also troubled by BEA's total lack of commitment to diversity and its willingness to look the other way when discrimination did occur. There had yet to be an African American in senior leadership. The Human Resource department seemed to lack any appreciation for Black employees.

For example, in 2005 BEA didn't recognize Black History Month (February) until February 25. In 2006 it was recognized on February 28. In 2007 it was recognized on February 17, but only because I wrote and submitted the article. This year it was recognized on the 26th. I didn't know if it was purposeful and spiteful or ignorance. I was convinced that had there been an African American in Human Resources or senior management, things would be much different.

It became increasingly difficult for me as I waited for DOE to render a decision on BEA's appeal. DeAnne had responded to BEA's appeal on October 6. A couple of weeks later we received an email from OHA that stated the case would be issued within sixty days. The estimated date was January 12, 2009. I could only hope and pray the decision would be made on or before that date.

Chapter 54: The Time Has Come

Every day at work seemed to get longer. Pretending to be an engineer was exhausting. I began taking more hours of vacation. With the presidential election getting closer, I became obsessed with following the campaigns. I sat mesmerized for each debate and followed the daily polling. I had little doubt that America would soon elect its first African American president. The conversations at work inevitably turned political. I was only one of a handful of Obama supporters. I enjoyed telling my Republican friends that the time had come.

LaVonna, Jasmine, and Darius were almost as excited as I was. On the evening of November 4, 2008, we gathered around the TV and watched the results come in. I had predicted it would be an early victory. At 9 p.m. NBC's Bryan Williams proclaimed, "And we have news. There will be young children in the White House for the first time since the Kennedy generation. An African American has broken the barrier as old as the republic, an astonishing candidate, an astonishing campaign, a seismic shift in American politics. You are looking at the 44th president of the United States; the celebrations begin."

The celebration had begun at our house. We high-fived, jumped, hugged, and shouted, "Yes we can." I never thought I would see this day.

Chapter 55: 2009 MLK Banquet

THE FIRST COUPLE OF WEEKS of 2009 went by slowly. The work days dragged on. My days were filled with meetings and procedure updates. There was nothing satisfying or rewarding about my work. The thing that kept me motivated was the upcoming Dr. King banquet on Saturday, January 19. Our keynote speaker was William Magwood IV. Bill had been the director of Nuclear Energy for DOE from 1998 through May 2005. Because of his close tie to the INL, we expected a large turnout of BEA senior managers.

The AAA had decided to invite the mayor of Rexburg, Idaho. Rexburg (twenty-five miles north of Idaho Falls) had been in the national news in November 2008 for a racially charged incident. The day after Barack Obama won the general election several children on a school bus had chanted, "Assassinate Obama." Obviously, these children were echoing the words of their parents. Yes, right there among us was this kind of hatred for our country's first African American president.

I picked up the phone and dialed the number of Rexburg's mayor.

"Mayor Larsen," he answered.

"Good afternoon; my name is Dennis Patterson, president of the African American Alliance."

The silence was deafening. I wasn't sure if he was still on the phone. I speculated he was worried that I was calling to discuss the chanting incident and perhaps even threaten legal action.

"Yes, how may I help you?" he finally responded.

"I'm calling to invite you to a banquet to honor Dr. King," I said.

"I would love to," he practically blurted out. The relief was evident in his voice.

A few days prior to the banquet, Grossenbacher's office asked for my help in arranging a meeting with Bill Magwood. For a moment, I was tempted to say 'thanks but no thanks.' Instead, I replied, "I'd be glad to."

BEA was more than willing to use my connection with an African American of importance, but had fought against my effort to help an African American construction worker.

The DOE–OHA appeal decision was due on Monday, January 12, but we still hadn't heard anything. The day before the banquet I was both anxious and excited. The next twenty-four hours could be life changing. Before going to work, I prayed for peace of mind and a calm spirit. The work day was fairly routine. I tried to stay focused on the work at hand, but my thoughts would return to the impending DOE decision. The decision was now three days past due. I thought about BEA senior management. Surely, they, too, were worried about the pending decision.

As lunch time approached, my cell phone rang and I anxiously looked at the caller ID. It was DeAnne's assistant, Brandi.

"We heard from the DOE Office of Hearings and Appeals," she said. I held my breath as I waited for the rest of the story. "DOE has given themselves an extension; the new date is February 10," she continued.

The disappointment was overwhelming. I thanked Brandi and ended the call. I took several deep breaths and tried to relax. It was so exasperating to have justice delayed once again. BEA's strategy had worked. They had overwhelmed DOE with paperwork. I called LaVonna and gave her the news.

"There must be a purpose beyond our understanding," she replied. She spoke with such conviction that it restored my confidence.

The next morning the AAA met with Magwood at Grandpa's Southern BBQ. Magwood expressed great interest in the AAA and our community. We discussed issues ranging from diversity to nuclear energy. After breakfast I drove him over to the INL and introduced him to Dr. Dave Hill, Deputy Laboratory Director for Science and Technology.

Later, I picked up Magwood and took him to the banquet. During the social hour I looked up and saw Grossenbacher. As he approached, he shook hands with Dave Snell. I watched as they chatted for a few minutes.

Grossenbacher walked toward me and extended his hand. We greeted each other with a firm grip.

"Great turnout, Dennis; thanks to you and Dave for putting this on."

"Thank you for coming," I replied.

Finally, after four long years, Grossenbacher and I had met face to face. This was our first opportunity to see each other as individuals rather than enemies engaged in mortal battle. I hoped this personal encounter might prompt Grossenbacher to intervene and try to end this horrific nightmare.

As the program kicked off, LaVonna and I took our places at the head table along with Magwood. Others at the table included Dr. Hill; Mayor Fuhriman and wife; John Kotek, former Deputy Manager DOE–ID and Ray Furstenau, Deputy Manager, DOE–ID.

At a table next to us were members of BEA senior

management, — Juan Alvarez, Art Clark, K.P. Ananth, and Grossenbacher.

One of the highlights for me came early in the program. Darius read Dr. King's, 'I Have a Dream' speech. I sat there proudly as he took the podium. In the background was video footage of Dr. King and the civil rights movement. It was such a special moment.

After the reading, Darius looked down at me. I gave him an approving nod and a smile. As I walked to the microphone, I was pleased to see the banquet room filled to capacity.

"Thank you all for being here to honor and celebrate Dr. King; it is my privilege to welcome you tonight," I began. I acknowledged the support of the mayors from the various cities and the numerous sponsors of the event.

I read my favorite Dr. King quote: "The ultimate measure of a man is not where he stands in times of comfort and convenience, but where he stands in times of challenge and controversy."

Ray Furstenau introduced Mr. Magwood. Upon taking the stage Magwood acknowledged the AAA and made a point of recognizing Darius' reading of Dr. King's speech.

Magwood's keynote address focused on the importance of education. He shared the time he visited classrooms in the Sun Valley area. He mentioned the state-of-the-art computers and instruction in Sun Valley and contrasted them with the run-down conditions of classrooms in Washington D.C.

He closed with, "America must do a better job providing the best education possible for all of its children."

Chapter 56: The Celebration

ON WEDNESDAY, JANUARY 21, 2009, DeAnne called. "I received a voice mail from BEA's outside counsel, Larry Halvorson."

"He said BEA would like to attempt to negotiate a settlement. I'm more than surprised that with only three weeks before the decision BEA wants to negotiate."

I told DeAnne that the offer likely came as a result of my meeting Grossenbacher at the Dr. King banquet.

"Maybe BEA wants to make things right or maybe save face with DOE. Let's see what they offer." DeAnne informed Halvorson that we would entertain an offer.

On February 4, after a long day at work I returned home. As I opened the door, my phone rang.

"We received a settlement offer from BEA, and I'm sending it via email now."

With my heart racing, I logged onto my computer and opened the email. The monetary offer was insulting and demeaning. If I accepted the offer, I would be left with fifty thousand dollars of attorney fees. A whole litany of profanities ran through my mind. BEA also refused to reinstate me as ethics officer. The final insult was they refused to even consider reassigning me from engineering to a more suitable position.

Most egregiously, the offer included a clause about BEA not admitting any guilt. How the hell could Olsen or Grossenbacher believe that after four years I would give up? That I would stop fighting to ensure that other employees wouldn't have to endure such treatment?

The next day DeAnne sent an email to Halvorson informing him we did not believe BEA was operating in good faith.

***

On the morning of February 10, I said my prayers and prepared for work. According to our last communication from DOE the appeal decision would be released today. As I left for work, I told LaVonna, "Love you, sweetheart; today is the day."

As the day wore on, I became increasingly anxious. By mid-afternoon I knew this would not be the day. When I got home, I collapsed onto the bed and just lay there thinking, *would this never end?*

DOE had failed to issue an extension and had communicated nothing to us about what was happening. At the end of the week, DeAnne sent an email and requested a status update. DOE said we should check back at the end of the following week. This cryptic message gave me hope that it wouldn't be much longer.

When I arrived at work on Monday morning, I passed by my old office. The door was ajar and I saw a middle-aged, heavy-set gentleman sitting at the desk. He looked up, smiled, and continued unpacking boxes. The sign on the door read, 'John Peterson.'

Later that morning, I sent DeAnne an email asking her to send an email to DOE requesting a status report. My patience was running out and the stress was overwhelming. When I came home from work, I logged onto my computer to see if we heard anything from DOE. I was disappointed to see that DeAnne hadn't sent the email to DOE.

The next day, March 10, 2009, I came home for lunch and checked my email. I had received an email from DeAnne. She told me she was reluctant to make an inquiry because the last time, DOE didn't seem too pleased and they hadn't suggested she check back. I told her I needed to hear something by the end of the week.

I lay on my bed watching TV. As the time came for me to go back to work, I didn't have the energy to even get off the bed. Finally, I decided to return and try to make it through the day. As I put on my coat, my cell phone rang. My pulse quickened when I saw the phone number.

"Hi, Dennis, this is DeAnne. The decision just came in." I held my breath as she continued. "DOE denied BEA's appeal in its entirety."

I was speechless but managed to utter "Wow." Chills ran through my body as I realized the enormity of the moment. DeAnne went on to say the wording of the report was more positive than the original report that had been issued in June 2008.

"Thank you for believing in me and the cause I was fighting for," I said.

"It was a pleasure," she responded. She said she would send me the report via email as soon as we hung up. But as fast as the internet is, I didn't have time to wait.

My first thought was that I needed to be with LaVonna. I hurriedly put on my coat, jumped in the car, and sped down to her office. The drive took me past the INL offices. I suspected that Mark Olsen was trying to figure out how to explain the loss to Grossenbacher.

When I arrived at LaVonna's office, the door was ajar so I barged in. She was standing at her desk. I had the biggest grin on my face as I greeted her. "We won," I declared. We grabbed each other and kissed. After nearly four years, it was over.

LaVonna went to her computer and opened DeAnne's email. We perused the report. It really was better than the first one.

The following excerpt was affirming: "Throughout its lengthy brief, BEA argues that the hearing officer ignored, misconstrued, or inaccurately described evidence. The hearing officer saw the witnesses testify, listened to the tapes of the two security office interviews of Patterson. She was thus in a position to consider the testimony and tape recordings in conjunction with the documentary evidence presented at the hearing. Most of the alleged errors are mere disagreements with the hearing officer's assessment of the testimony, evidence, and credibility of the witnesses. The hearing officer's findings in this regard are clearly not erroneous and will be allowed to stand. Any actual hearing officer errors are insignificant."

BEA had alleged that the hearing officer had made sixty errors in her decision. The appeal decision did not validate a single one. I had never seen a more overwhelming and decisive defeat.

The appeal ruling also took issue with the fact that it was the Security office that investigated me. "Patterson's 2005 investigation found the Security office guilty of deficiencies that resulted in corrective action. Patterson's allegations of the security office and BEA management of unethical behavior led to a review of the security office by Battelle Memorial Institute."

As I'd always believed, it was wrong and inappropriate for the organization I found guilty of wrongdoing to conduct investigations of me. Yet that is what Middleton had authorized repeatedly.

After a few moments of celebrating, I told LaVonna I had to return to work. Upon arriving at work, the first thing I did was send an email to friends and family. I informed everyone that I had won, again. I closed with the words, "God is good."

That evening LaVonna and I celebrated at our favorite restaurant, the Sandpiper. It is where I proposed to her in 2004. We sat on the deck overlooking the Snake River. The evening was a special time of celebrating and giving thanks.

Chapter 57: An Illusion

MARCH 11, 2009, the *Post Register* ran a story, "Doe Whistleblower Case Closed." The headline was quite disappointing to me for two reasons. First, the wording did not indicate who prevailed in the case, only that it was closed. Second, it was no longer front-page news. Only the dedicated reader would take the time to read the article and grasp the true impact and importance of DOE's decision.

BEA's response to the decision was shameful, but predictable. In 2008 Mark Olsen and Grossenbacher had sent an iNote to all employees stating they disagreed with the decision that they had retaliated against me and were appealing. This time, after losing the appeal, BEA communicated nothing to employees.

No acknowledgement of outcome.

No acknowledgement of wrongdoing.

Nothing. It was as if it never happened.

A few days later, I visited with a friend in the Internal Audit division. I discovered that Benson had returned to the laboratory and was now director of International Audits. Benson had served his six months of 'professional development' at Battelle Corporate and returned to what appeared to be a promotion. Prior to leaving, he was the director of Internal Audit. I couldn't help but believe this was another example of white privilege. Would an African American under the same circumstances be treated with such forgiveness, kindness, and generosity? Benson could now finish out his INL career and retire with full benefits. I wondered if I would be given the same opportunity. Of course, in my heart I was pretty damn sure I wouldn't.

Chapter 58: Good, Bad and Ugly

I RECEIVED NUMEROUS CONGRATULATORY EMAILS. One in particular caught my attention. It was sent by a prominent community leader, Sheila Olsen. She and I shared a close friend, Americus John-Lewis (AJ). Sheila sent me the following message: "Congratulations Dennis! What a wonderful example of faith, courage, perseverance, patience, and standing for right this is! I am so happy for you and so proud to call you my friend."

Years earlier, AJ, a devout Roman Catholic and Sheila, a devout Mormon, had put together a 24-hour multi-denominational prayer-a-thon. To be congratulated and recognized by Sheila was quite special. I suspected that AJ was looking down from heaven with a smile.

My pastor wrote, "This has been a long hard struggle, but through the process you have blessed others along the journey in ways you can't imagine." These words of inspiration from the leader of my spiritual life were very humbling. Other messages received included:

"This is great news; it gives hope to all that we do."

"I am glad justice was finally served."

"You and your family have been in our thoughts and prayers. I did so pray for this to happen."

"Praise the Lord." (several emails contained this message)

"Halleluiah!!" (one of my favorites)

Every morning when I woke up it was easier to get out of bed. Taking a shower was more pleasurable, the coffee tasted better, and the sun seemed to shine brighter. Life was good!

A few days after I won the appeal, I received an invitation from Grossenbacher's office. The invitation simply said, "Discussion with Dennis Patterson."

Finally, after more than four years, I was getting the opportunity to meet with him. The good feeling lasted only seconds. I noticed that Grossenbacher had also invited Mark Olsen to the meeting.

Back in 2005, when I told Olsen I wanted a meeting with Grossenbacher, he tried to intimidate me by barking, "Do you really want to take me on?" Olsen had been part of the ongoing harassment and retaliation. I accepted the meeting invitation but requested that Olsen not attend and explained my reasons. I told Grossenbacher, if a senior manager needed to be present, I recommended Dr. Harold Blackman.

Approximately a week later, Grossenbacher wrote back and informed me Olsen would not be attending. The meeting was scheduled for April 3, 2009.

As the meeting day approached my feelings fluctuated between excitement and anticipation to dread and anxiety. The morning of the meeting I read Scriptures, prayed, and took notes of what I wanted to say. As I entered Grossenbacher's office, I saw Harold Blackman. Grossenbacher met me at the door and shook my hand. As we sat at the table the tension was palpable.

John began, "Dennis, you are a valued employee. I wanted to give you a chance to meet with me. The whistleblower case is over. I want our conversation to focus on the future. What do you have to say?"

I thanked him and began, "John, as a long-time employee and a native of Idaho Falls, I am committed to the success of the laboratory. I filed the whistleblower complaint because I believed that in the end it would help make the INL a better place to work. We have to create a work environment where employees feel valued and respected."

We discussed issues including safety, pension plan, diversity, retention, attrition, and senior leadership. After about forty-five minutes, John closed his folder and moved away from the table as though to say the meeting was over. For me, the meeting wasn't over. John had said nothing about my career.

The DOE report issued on March 9, 2009, recommended that BEA consider reinstating me to the ethics officer position. It also directed, as an alternative, for BEA to identify a 'comparable position.' As John rose to leave, he asked, "Is there anything else?' I'm sure he expected me to say no. Of course, since he invited me to talk, I would talk. I was not going to rely on bureaucracy and legal maneuvering to determine my fate.

"Yes, John, there is something else. I would like to talk about my career." I watched his face. He couldn't have been more stoic. It was as if he was void of feelings or emotion.

"You are like any other employee. If you see a job opening, apply for it; if you get it great, if not keep trying," he said. I was stunned by his response. The idea that he would say I was just like any other employee was very hurtful. BEA had intimidated, harassed, and taken retribution against me. I had been investigated multiple times, unfairly escorted from the premises of the INL, and removed from the job I loved.

I pulled up my chair closer and replied, "John, we seem to have a different understanding of the DOE report. I believe that BEA has a responsibility to find me a comparable job." He remained stoic.

"Have you read the DOE report?" I asked.

"I haven't read it in detail, but I will and then we'll meet again. You may not like what I say, but we'll talk again."

He quickly retracted the latter remark and said, "Well, let's just say I'll give you a response." He asked, "Is that fair?"

"Yes," was all I could say.

We stood and shook hands. I looked at Harold, who had remained silent throughout the meeting. As we exited, Harold asked, "How are you doing, Dennis?"

"Fine," I replied. Of course, I wasn't fine, and I'm sure he knew it. I hadn't expected an apology but I didn't expect Grossenbacher to act as though nothing had happened. As though my life and career didn't matter.

***

I was in regular communications with DeAnne. She had been speaking with Larry Halvorson about the details of the decision and trying to reach a final resolution. The major sticking point appeared to be DOE's recommendation that BEA consider placing me back in the Ethics Office or finding a comparable position. Every action taken by BEA over the past four years indicated they would never do this.

We soon learned we were right. Mark Olsen had informed DOE Office of Hearings and Appeals that they would not reinstate me, nor would they find another position for me. They argued, and convinced DOE OHA, that my current position in engineering was 'comparable' and therefore no further action was necessary. BEA also argued that they had already hired someone to fill the ethics position and it would create a hardship on him.

I was infuriated, not only at BEA but also the DOE Office of Hearings and Appeals. I considered writing directly to the DOE Energy Secretary, Dr. Steven Chu. Refusing to put me back in the office or finding a comparable job was not only unfair but wholly inconsistent with providing protections to whistleblowers.

Another point of contention arose when Mark Olsen and Katherine Moriarty sent me an email informing me that BEA would not remove my unjust 2006 performance appraisal from my personnel file. How could they refuse to follow a direct and unambiguous order from the hearing officer?

I decided to send an email to Juan Alvarez asking him to intervene. Within twenty-four hours the appraisal was removed from my file. I was shocked. A BEA senior manager had made the right decision and it didn't take forever to do so.

A rewarding moment came near the end of the process. I went down to DeAnne's office to take care of a little paperwork. BEA had submitted the check to pay my attorney fees. The check was in excess of eighty thousand dollars. I signed the check over to Holden, Hahn, Kidwell, and Crapo. The relief was physical, mental, and emotional. I hadn't fully appreciated how heavy the financial burden had been. But now this part was over. No more worries about losing our home or paying for the kids' college education. At least for now.

Chapter 59: Ghost from the Past

Days after my meeting with Grossenbacher, I received an email from Juan Alvarez, Deputy Laboratory Director for Management. He and Mark Holubar, Human Resource Director, wanted to meet with me to discuss my future. This gave me a feeling of hope and excitement. Of course, the good feeling was tempered by the fact that Alvarez had written the letter in 2005 that questioned my fitness to be ethics officer.

I entered Alvarez's office. Juan greeted me with a smile and a handshake.

"I've read the DOE report and I believe this is the right thing to do. We are not doing this because we have to; we are doing it because we believe it is best for everyone," Juan said.

Holubar said BEA wanted to create a job that would leverage my skills, experience, and abilities. At the end of the meeting, Holubar mentioned a personality profile questionnaire. "Dennis, we want you to take the Hogan Assessment."

I immediately became suspicious and asked, "How many BEA employees have taken this assessment?"

"None," Holubar replied.

"Well, I'm not comfortable being the first, especially under the circumstances," I replied.

Alvarez interrupted, "Dennis, take a couple of days and think about it."

In my opinion, having me take a personality profile was another example of BEA treating me differently than other employees. Why should a Black man have his personality and character questioned? Battelle corporate and DOE had already made affirmative assessments of my competency, character, and abilities.

Later that evening, LaVonna and I discussed whether I should take the personality profile. In the final analysis, I really didn't have much choice. If I declined, Holubar and Alvarez would likely use my refusal as an excuse to keep me in engineering.

The next time I met with them, I said I would take the assessment. The following week I completed the several page questionnaire. The subject areas included business philosophy, leadership style, personal attributes, and ethics. A few days after completing the assessment I spent three hours on the phone with a Battelle corporate officer reviewing the results. Overall, I was very pleased with the outcome. The report identified 'ethics' as an area of strength for me.

Two weeks later I again met with Juan and Mark. This time they had a formal position description and offered me the job. I would report directly to Juan with responsibility for developing a manager workshop and leading a new laboratory initiative to measure and improve employee engagement. The job required regular interface and coordination with senior leadership.

Juan also committed to providing me with a private office, comparable to the one I had as ethics officer. Juan gave me a copy of the job description and asked me to let him know if I would accept within a couple of days.

On the surface this appeared to be a great opportunity, but I had one serious reservation. One thing was almost a certainty. If budgets became tight, this would become one of the first positions to be eliminated. Additionally, being a whistleblower put a target on my back. It was unlikely I could find another job there at the laboratory or perhaps anywhere.

Nonetheless, LaVonna and I agreed that I would accept the position.

I readily acclimated to the new job and new surroundings. Unfortunately, the surroundings didn't include a private office as promised. I was placed in a cubicle, this time without a window.

***

The summer of 2009 was relaxing and exciting. The relief could be felt every night when I went to sleep and every morning when I awoke. The excitement of a job I enjoyed sometimes felt too good to be true.

One of my primary job duties was leading a new BEA initiative. BEA had recently decided to contract with the Gallup Corporation to conduct annual all-employee surveys. The purpose was to measure 'employee engagement.' Engagement surveys measured the employees' emotional and psychological commitment to the company. I found it quite ironic that a former whistleblower would be leading this effort.

During the month of July, approximately 80 percent of all employees voluntarily participated in the anonymous survey. Senior management was anxious to get the results, though they did not expect them to be very good. In September, Gallup sent us the survey results. The overall score placed BEA in the bottom 15 percent when compared to other national laboratories. In many ways, I felt vindicated. The results let me know I was not alone in my views of BEA and the work environment.

Managers were required to share organizational results with their employees and collaborate with them to identify actions to improve the work environment. I led a team of employees responsible for providing direction, making recommendations to management, and facilitating employee discussions.

In late fall, I heard rumors that Mark Olsen was leaving the laboratory. This didn't surprise me. Olsen had played a primary role in the retaliation and the failed defense of my whistleblower complaint. I hoped the rumors of his departure were true. It would be best for BEA and best for BEA employees. However, I didn't know if 'leaving the laboratory' meant he was being terminated or simply being transferred to another Battelle facility. I suspected the latter.

My other main job assignment was development and deployment of a management workshop called "Mandate to Manage." The workshop included the key operational areas of the lab including finance, legal, safety, human resources, audit, and the four mission areas.

The modules were taught by the senior manager of each function. The pilot was successfully launched. It signaled a successful beginning to my new career at the INL.

Chapter 60: "Learning, Earning, Returning"

AS WINTER APPROACHED, I was busy helping to plan the 2010 Dr. King banquet. The AAA decided to invite Dr. Pete Miller to be the keynote speaker. Miller had just been nominated by President Obama to be director of Nuclear Energy for the Department of Energy. Miller was confirmed, and became the person responsible for oversight and management of the INL.

Some believed we had zero chance of getting an acceptance because it was the dead of winter in Idaho. Surely, Miller would have more enticing speaking opportunities. Nonetheless, we prepared an invitation letter. I sent it via email from my office at 11:25 a.m. and then left to meet LaVonna for lunch. At 11:43 a.m. my blackberry beeped. I opened up my email and was pleased to read, "I would be honored to speak at your event."

The banquet was held on Friday, January 15. Seated at the head table was Dr. Miller; Michelle Scott, his assistant; John Grossenbacher and his wife, Kathy; Dennis Miotla, acting DOE–ID manager; and LaVonna and me. LaVonna looked stunning in her new green dress. After Dr. Miller recognized distinguished guests he commented, "Dennis Patterson has become a new friend and so has his lovely wife." This was a proud moment for me.

During Dr. Miller's keynote address we learned that as a child one of his good friends was Emmett Till. That fateful summer in 1955, Pete Miller, fourteen-years-old, was living in Chicago.

Emmett's family had invited Pete to go with them on a family vacation to Mississippi. Pete's mother, aware of the dangers of the south, refused to let Pete go with his friend, the same age as Pete. History tells us the rest of the story. While in Mississippi, two white men beat Emmett and dumped his body in the Tallahatchie River with a cotton gin fan tied around his neck with barbed wire. The audience gasped upon hearing a story that until now was just words in a history book.

Miller closed with, "I would like to leave you with advice I learned from my father a long time ago. You should spend your life one third learning, one third earning, and one third returning." Weeks after the banquet folks were still talking about Dr. Miller's talk and the profound impact it had on them.

***

One morning, shortly after arriving at work I received a call from Juan's administrator. "Dennis, Juan wants to see you right away."

Juan greeted me and closed the door. "Dennis, I would like you to go to Washington D.C for a two-week assignment."

"I would love to," I said, before even knowing the details.

"This is a professional development opportunity; it will benefit you as well as the laboratory," Juan said.

My assignment would include attending congressional budget hearings and possibly meetings with Idaho congressional representatives Mike Simpson and Mike Crapo. Almost as an afterthought Juan added, "It will also be a great opportunity for you to visit with Pete Miller."

I wasn't surprised at all that BEA would take the opportunity to leverage my relationship with Miller. And of course, it didn't hurt that I was African American. BEA still did not have an African American in senior leadership.

As the meeting came to a close, Juan shifted in his chair. Almost painfully, he brought up the subject of my whistleblower complaint.

"Dennis, I regret sending the letter to Benson back when all this started. If I had a problem with you, I should have invited you to my office and talked to you. Maybe we could have worked it through and perhaps avoided all this."

I almost fell out of my chair. "Yes, that would have been better. The letter damaged my reputation and it felt like retaliation. Why didn't you talk to me later?"

"Because Olsen advised me to have no communication with you. If there is one lesson I've learned, it's that a company should never forget that the employee is still a person, not just a whistleblower."

I realized this was the closest thing to an apology that I would ever get. However, Juan's 'regret' was not the same as accepting responsibility or accountability. But I agreed with Juan's statement that he and others had forgotten I was a person. I had been dehumanized in the same manner as Loren Mitchell. Two African Americans who had done nothing wrong, yet had been victimized by those in power and authority.

On March 22nd I found myself on a plane to Washington D.C. Almost exactly a year before I had won my whistleblower complaint. For two weeks, I stayed at the W Hotel across the street from the White House. I attended hearings, breakfast meetings, and met senior DOE and Battelle managers. I was tempted to stop by the office of Hearing Officer, Adeyeye, but decided against it because I wasn't sure of the protocol. However, I was sure she would have enjoyed hearing 'the rest of the story.'

Chapter 61: An American Hero

ON MY LAST DAY IN D. C. I decided to walk the halls of Congress. I noticed an office with the name 'Representative John Lewis, Georgia.' I had always admired and respected John Lewis. I remembered him marching with Dr. King. I remembered him being beaten, arrested, and jailed. I knew he had spent his life fighting for fairness, justice, and equality. Just as I had shaken Obama's hand in 2008, I wanted to shake John Lewis' hand.

I entered the reception area. "Good afternoon, my name is Dennis Patterson. I'm from Idaho and I'm wondering if there is any chance I could shake Congressman Lewis' hand?"

"Yes, of course, I'm sure he would love to meet you. Please have a seat."

A few minutes later Mr. Lewis came out, smiled, and extended his hand. "Good afternoon. Welcome; please come into my office."

His office was large and spacious, befitting someone who had served twelve terms in the U.S. House of Representatives. The room was filled with historical documents, newspapers, and pictures that told of the civil rights struggle. There was a picture of the August 28, 1963, March on Washington.

"Dennis, as you may know, I gave a speech that day as chair of the Student Nonviolent Coordinating Committee. I was only twenty-three-years-old. King taught all of us how to speak up and speak out whenever there is injustice," he said.

I responded, "Dr. King has been my hero since I was a little boy. A few years ago, I helped organize a community non-profit, the African American Alliance. We are trying to make our community better. Each year we honor Dr. King with a banquet in Idaho Falls."

"Tell your organization thank you for what it is doing," he responded.

At the end of our visit he summoned a staffer to take a picture of us shaking hands on the balcony of his office, with the U.S Capitol in the background.

"Thank you for your courage and sacrifice for our country," I said.

As I walked out of his office, I wasn't sure my feet were touching the ground. I felt as though I had journeyed with Dr. King. I had met and visited with an American hero.

***

After a year working to improve the work environment, BEA senior management was optimistic that the results from the 2010 Gallup survey would be more positive. The results were released in October. The improvement was significant. INL had gone from being in the bottom 15 percent compared to other labs to the 35th percentile. According to Gallup, this was one of the largest one-year increases they had seen for a large institution like the INL. As the person responsible for managing the Gallup survey and the follow-up efforts to improve the workplace, I found this very gratifying.

***

Our friends Joy and Kirk Wilkie invited us to join their prayer group. Pastor Bob and his wife Mary Beth were part of the group. Bob and Mary Beth exemplified love, compassion, and unwavering faith. On Saturday mornings we met at a local coffee shop and discussed inspirational Christian books and prayed for each other. No matter the situation or circumstance, LaVonna and I always left the bistro feeling blessed and encouraged by our dear friends.

Professionally, this was the first year since 2004 that I wasn't in the midst of challenge and controversy. In my annual performance review with Alvarez I received praise and recognition for my contributions to the success of the INL. As I prepared to leave his office he handed me an envelope and said, "Job well done."

I waited until I returned to my office to open it. Inside was a commendation letter: "We appreciate your individual contributions to the laboratory's on-going success. It is only through efforts like yours that we will transform the INL into the preeminent laboratory and help solve America's energy challenges. Congratulations and thank you."

Along with the commendation letter was a check. Yes indeed, it had been a very good year!

Chapter 62: Dr. King Banquets

IT WAS TIME for the 2011 Dr. Martin Luther King banquet. This year we were fortunate to have a very special keynote speaker — Dr. Debbie Thomas. At this point, I was no longer president of the African American Alliance. After the 2010 banquet I had decided it was time to step down. My good friend, David Snell, assumed the presidency.

Prior to the banquet Debbie held an autograph session at the local hockey shelter. It was a pleasure watching her visit with the youth as she signed autographs and posed for pictures. Many of these same kids came to the banquet.

In her keynote address, Debbie spoke about being a young child with a dream of becoming a champion figure skater and a doctor and how she had succeeded at both. She won the World Figure Skating Championship and was the first African American to win a medal in the Winter Olympics, winning the bronze medal in figure skating in 1988. She got her medical degree in 1997 and served her residency at the Martin Luther King/Charles Drew University Medical Center in South Central Los Angeles.

Dr. Thomas' message was inspiring to young and old alike.

***

The 2012 Dr. King banquet featured Bruce Smith as the keynote speaker. Bruce was a senior animator for Disney films. He had supervised animation on *Tarzan*, *The Emperor's New Groove*, *Princess and the Frog*, and *Winnie the Pooh*.

He was also the creator and producer of the *Proud Family*, a Disney animated TV sitcom about a fourteen-year-old African American girl and her family. Bruce was a very engaging and entertaining speaker. He shared his personal story of trials, tribulations, and successes as a trailblazer in the animated film industry. He spoke about the need for greater diversity and how he used people from his life experience in characters he had animated. He encouraged the children to pursue their dreams with hard work and determination. He closed with, "Thank you, Idaho Falls, for bringing me out here; this is a beautiful place. We are all family, young and old." The crowd was delighted by his inspiring and hopeful keynote presentation.

For me, it was another example of the importance of having African Americans in positions of influence. Smith was breaking new ground in creating characters that children of color could relate to. His personal journey helped children realize they, too, could achieve their dreams.

Also on the program was the Honorable Cherie Buckner-Webb, Idaho's first African American state legislator and co-founder of Idaho's Black History Museum in Boise. During her remarks she told the audience, "You have a charge to keep." She explained that this was an old-time phrase that means we still have work to do. She added, "If anyone lives in injustice, we all live in injustice." Cherie added to the evening's enjoyment with a beautiful rendition of, "He Looked Beyond My Faults."

The banquet was a great success. The African American Alliance was privileged to present a check for $2,500 to a local non-profit, HELP Inc., an organization committed to fighting child abuse and assisting families in crisis.

Chapter 63: The Sun is Setting

LATE IN FEBRUARY 2012 I met with Juan to discuss my performance for 2011 and my goals and objectives for 2012.

Juan began, "Your performance for 2011 met all my expectations." He then added, "Dennis, you have the right skills and abilities to do well in the Labor Relations division. I would like you to spend at least two months working in labor relations. I want you to learn the function and operations of the department. This may be a viable career path for you."

I didn't know for sure, but I sensed that the unspoken message was that my current job was in jeopardy and Juan was looking for a way to move me to another department.

I responded, "I look forward to the opportunity and the challenge." Juan said he would set up a meeting with the Labor Relations manager, Mark Wangler, to make this happen.

On March 25, 2012, Juan and I met with Wangler. During the forty-minute meeting, thirty-five minutes Wangler talked about his own successes and triumphs in the labor relations world. In the final five minutes, Juan explained to Wangler his intention to have me spend time in his department.

"Sure, Juan, we can make this happen. Dennis, contact me next week and we'll get together," Wangler said.

The next week I sent Wangler an email referencing our meeting with Juan and my availability to meet any time. I heard nothing from Wangler over the next two weeks. I sent him a reminder on April 30. Again, I heard nothing. On May 14, I sent another email. Still no response. It had been eight weeks. I concluded that Wangler had no intention of meeting with me or allowing me anywhere near his department.

I suspected that Wangler had found out I was a whistleblower. He may have even felt like Juan was trying to pull one over on him. Of course, all of this was just conjecture on my part. The only thing I knew for certain was that after repeated attempts to communicate with him, I didn't even receive the courtesy of a "thanks but no thanks."

After not hearing from Wangler for several weeks I contacted his boss, Director of Human Resources, Mark Holubar. Holubar said he didn't know anything about this, but would follow-up and get back to me. How could he not know? Juan was Holubar's boss and Wangler reported to Holubar.

Since it was clear BEA had no interest in furthering my career, I chose to make the best of a difficult situation. A year before, the INL decided to sponsor the first ever INL Toastmaster club. I had joined, hopeful that one day I could begin a new career giving speeches to inspire and motivate others.

On May 12, 2012, Toastmasters District 15, which included Idaho, Utah, Nevada, and Oregon, held the annual speech contest in Salt Lake City. I participated in the 'Table Topics' category. This competition tests a person's ability to give a short speech on the spot without any preparation.

When my turn came, I was introduced and given the question, "If you could interview anyone past or present, who would it be and what would you ask?"

Without pausing, I said it would be Dr. Martin Luther King Jr. Instinctively, I reflected back to 2006 when I participated on a diversity panel in Idaho Falls. I was asked my opinion on whether Dr. King would support the right of gays to be married.

"Dr. King would oppose gay marriage because he was a minister and the Bible teaches that homosexuality is a sin," is how I responded in 2006.

But today I no longer believed this. Here in the midst of perhaps the most conservative city in America I responded, "I believe that if asked, Dr. King would say he supports gay marriage, because it is a matter of equality and fairness."

I knew that saying this could jeopardize my chance to win the competition, but I plunged ahead. As I spoke, I looked in the eyes of the audience members. To my surprise, I could see compassion and understanding.

I returned to my seat and sat next to Jasmine to await the announcement of the winner.

"And the first-place winner is … Dennis Patterson."

As I accepted the trophy, I was proud to have spoken truth. Jasmine gave me a big. "Dad, I'm so proud of you." Later she told me she had gotten a tattoo. It was a quote from Maya Angelou, "In diversity there is beauty and strength." I was proud of my daughter for recognizing the value of all people.

On July 18, 2012, there was a special INL ceremony in honor of a friend, Mary Dee Grimm. She had reached her fifty-year anniversary with the INL and it was my privilege to attend the celebration. Mary Dee represented the best of the INL — outstanding work ethic, honesty, integrity, and highly respected by colleagues and staff.

Holubar was present at the ceremony, but for most of the event he avoided me. It had been four months since Juan had talked to me about working in Labor Relations/Human Resources. When I finally got his attention, before even saying hello, Holubar said, "Hey

Dennis, I talked to Wangler; he said he would have to get back to me." By this time I was convinced this whole thing was a farce. There was going to be no professional development opportunity for me.

"No problem, Mark; just let me know," I said with resignation. The lack of integrity was disheartening but no longer a surprise.

Later in August, I met with Juan.

"Dennis, as you know the budget is going to be real tight this year and there will likely be more layoffs. Would you be willing to relocate if the right job came along?"

I knew what this meant. My career at the INL was coming to an end. "Of course, Juan; I'd enjoy a new challenge."

"Great, I'll be talking to managers at other Battelle sites and see what I can make happen." I was hopeful that Juan was being sincere, but I had my doubts.

That evening I shared the news with LaVonna. She was hopeful. "You know, if someone at Juan's level wants it to happen, it will happen."

Over the next several weeks, LaVonna and I talked about the possibility of living in a different city. We were excited, but knew nothing would happen unless Juan really wanted it to.

In late October, I met with Juan as a follow-up to our August meeting. From the outset there was a different tone than our previous discussion. Juan again noted the INL budget problems and its potential impact on the workforce.

"All of the Battelle operations are facing similar budget challenges," he emphasized.

I didn't say much. Toward the end of the meeting, Juan added, "At our next meeting we need to revisit the issue of your professional development and your future."

"Okay, I'll come prepared with some ideas and proposals," I said.

Chapter 64: America's First Lady

In early August LaVonna, Dave Snell, and I drove to Jackson Hole, Wyoming to see Michelle Obama speak at a fundraising event. By arriving early we were able to stand within twenty feet of where she was speaking.

Michelle's speech was uplifting and inspiring, especially when she spoke about the importance of educating our youth and our responsibility as parents. After her talk, she walked along the rope line and began shaking hands. The first hand she shook was Dave's. He was so surprised that he was speechless for perhaps the first time in his life.

A few minutes later she clasped LaVonna's hand and smiled. LaVonna beamed as her eyes met Michelle's.

"Tell the President thank you for all he is doing for our country," she said. I was next to shake Michelle's hand.

"God Bless and thank you," I said. The opportunity to speak to the First Lady was an experience that LaVonna and I will never forget. For me, it brought back memories of shaking the hand of Michelle's husband, aka President Obama, back in 2008. I was living a truly charmed and blessed life.

Chapter 65: Almost Sundown

For my scheduled November meeting with Juan, I came prepared with a one-page 'white paper.' It highlighted my experience, education, and contributions to the success of the INL. I also identified specific INL jobs that I was qualified for and interested in. I included the employee concerns program manager and ethics officer positions. Until now, I had never explicitly stated an interest in these jobs because I believed that BEA would never consider me. However, at this point I had nothing to lose.

In the white paper I also included the possibility of being the manager of the diversity or employee relations (ER) division. I handed the paper to Juan at the beginning of our meeting. He glanced at it, but left it on the table and began writing on his whiteboard. This gave me the impression that his mind was already made up.

"Dennis, you don't have the breadth and depth of experience to manage an ER function, and diversity is no longer a focus area for Battelle."

"So, what about going back to do what I used to do?" I asked.

"I don't think that would work," he responded. Juan was careful not to mention why it wouldn't work.

For most of the meeting, I was trying to absorb what all of this meant. I concluded that Juan was preparing the groundwork for laying me off. I wondered if this would be our last meeting.

The week before Christmas, during a management workshop, I visited with John Peterson. John was hired as the employee concerns program (ECP) manager in March 2009. More recently, he had been transferred to supervisor of audits. I asked John if he missed being the ECP manager. "Sometimes," he responded. He talked about his first days at the INL. As he had told me once before, on his second day of employment he picked up the newspaper and read that I had won the appeal of my whistleblower complaint.

"To this day, I am still angry no one told me about the pending complaint prior to being hired. Had I known I would have never accepted the job," he said.

It had been almost four years since John was hired as the ECP manager and he still remembered this event like it was yesterday. He also told me that when he was hired, he had no relevant experience for the job.

In my thirty-two years at the INL I was not aware of a single African American who had been hired with no relevant experience for the job. Of course, I had been involuntarily transferred to an engineering job with no experience, but in my case, I believed it was done with the expectation and hope that I would fail.

I was looking forward to the week off between Christmas and New Year's. The stress of the impending layoff and the conversations with Juan made for long days at work. On December 20, 2012, management released an iNote. The note told employees what we already knew. There would be a layoff in early 2013.

Chapter 66:

2012 MLK Banquet — "I Challenge You"

THIS YEAR WE WERE FORTUNATE to have as our keynote speaker, Dr. Freeman Hrabowski III, President, University Maryland Baltimore County. In 2012, *TIME* magazine had named Hrabowski "One of the 100 most influential people in the world." At the age of twelve, Freeman had been arrested and jailed for twelve days for participating in a children's civil rights march with Dr. King.

The morning of the banquet, Freeman had breakfast with members of the African American Alliance at the Wasabi Grill. He encouraged the young people in attendance to consider majoring in math, science, and engineering. At the end of the breakfast, he gave Jasmine and another young lady a math problem and challenged them to have the correct answer by the time of the banquet. To his delight, and mine, both girls gave him the right answer just prior to his keynote address.

The audience was enthralled with Dr. Hrabowski's keynote address. He began with, "My message is very simple. The way we think about ourselves as a country, as a community, here in Idaho Falls, as individuals and families, the way we talk about ourselves, the language that we use, the values that we hold will be so important. We become those things; they determine our destiny."

Freeman spoke about the importance of math, science, and

engineering, especially for our children. He said, "The challenge is to help children of all races get that education. If they get the education, all things are possible."

He commented about Idaho Falls. "This is a community where people care about each other. Here is a community where you have a Dr. King celebration and you have all races here, because they believe in it and believe in themselves."

He closed with the following: "I challenge you, Idaho Falls, to watch your thoughts, they become your words; watch your words because they become your actions; watch your actions because they become your habits; and watch your habits because they become your character. Character becomes destiny, dreams, and values. Idaho Falls, you are a very special community and you can become even better."

This was another great event hosted by the Idaho Falls African American Alliance. It was a unique opportunity to hear from an African American who had fought for civil rights and had gone on to achieve the highest level of success. Dr. Hrabowski was an American hero in every sense of the word. I was thrilled that Jasmine and the other young people had the privilege of meeting him and hearing his call to action. For the rest of us, no one is exempt from the challenge to do better and be better.

Chapter 67: Full Circle

On Sunday, February 13 LaVonna and I attended church as usual. At the close of his sermon, Pastor Bob informed us that several members of a family would be baptized. He asked the family to gather around the baptismal pool at the front of the sanctuary. To my surprise and delight Loren Mitchell and his wife Michelle went forward.

Bob baptized five of their children. At the conclusion of the baptism Bob invited friends to congratulate the family. LaVonna and I went forward and gave Loren and his wife a hug and wished God's blessings upon them.

In my heart, I knew this was meant to be part of my story. It wasn't by chance or happenstance that Loren had called the BEA hotline almost exactly eight years ago. Loren had been placed in my path for a reason. I was a better person for having gone through the experience.

Chapter 68: The Last Mile

THE WEEK OF MARCH 4TH I spent time doing a goodbye tour. I stopped by the offices of friends and colleagues. I told them I would be laid off within the next few days. It was difficult saying good bye. For all its challenges, the INL is a place filled with great people doing great work. I would miss being part of the INL family.

Tuesday morning, March 12, I awoke shortly before 7 a.m. and prepared for work. I checked my iPhone. Exactly at 7 a.m. an iNote was delivered to all employees: "Involuntary separations will begin today." I woke up LaVonna. "Sweetheart, today is the day."

Before leaving, LaVonna and I prayed together. "I love you, God will be with you," she said.

I arrived at my desk at 8 a.m. At 8:10 a.m. my phone rang.

"Juan needs to meet with you right away," Kelli, Juan's assistant, said.

I called LaVonna. "I just got the call, I'll be home soon."

I entered Juan's office; the tension was palpable. I could hear Juan's labored breathing as he prepared to speak. I took a seat at the round table. Juan took a seat on the other side, a little farther away than usual. We had sat at this table many times over the past three years.

This was nothing like those meetings. Juan's voice was strained as he began the obviously well-rehearsed script. It took less than sixty seconds.

"As part of a skill set realignment required to perform our mission efficiently within the levels of funding provided by various customers, there is a need to reduce INL's workforce through an Involuntary Separation process. Your position is impacted by this reduction and is being eliminated. Can I or Kelli help you with packing or taking stuff to your car?"

"No thanks, I have already taken everything home except for my family picture."

Juan was surprised that I knew I was being laid off and that I had taken all necessary actions. "Is there anything I can do?" he asked.

"No thanks, it's finished." We shook hands and I left his office.

I returned to my cubicle to get my personal effects and say a final goodbye to friends and colleagues. The first thing I did was retrieve two draft emails I had prepared. The first was addressed to approximately two hundred employees.

"Well, it's been a long journey here at the laboratory. I feel blessed to have been part of this great institution and even more blessed to have known each of you. Today is my last day as an INL employee. While a bit sad, I leave knowing that God will continue to lead my life and bless me with new challenges and opportunities. I wish and pray the best for the laboratory. Always remember: Faith, Family, Friends."

A good friend, Sammy Tawfik, responded, "Your kindness and life example were light for so many around the lab. I will miss you around here. But I hope to see you when you can and learn from you how God continues to use you. Best wishes to you."

The second email I addressed to approximately fifteen colleagues. As a group, with the support of senior management, we had developed a set of 'INL Values.'

These values were intended to provide the foundation for improved decision making and help build trust within INL. The four values were: Integrity, Excellence, Teamwork, and Ownership. Juan and I had several conversations about the values. He had expressed his personal commitment to them. The values had been approved by Grossenbacher and were ready to be communicated to all employees.

The roll-out of the values was scheduled for April. Grossenbacher was to personally endorse the values and express BEA's commitment to them.

Herein was the problem. In the opinion of many, including me, Grossenbacher was no longer the right person to communicate the values. During the past couple of weeks, a rumor was rampant throughout the laboratory. The rumor was that Grossenbacher had failed to live up to the values he himself had approved.

My concern was not with the truthfulness of the rumor; my concern was that most employees seemed to believe the rumor. In my email, I suggested that someone other than Grossenbacher should endorse and communicate the values.

This email was my last official act as an INL employee. As I experienced this surreal moment, it was not lost on me that BEA was violating these very values. First, BEA had never accepted ownership of its unlawful and unfair treatment of me. Second, the decision to terminate me did not demonstrate integrity, excellence, or teamwork. A total of 101 employees were laid off out of approximately 3500. It was beyond comprehension that BEA couldn't have found an opportunity for me, a thirty-three-year employee with an outstanding performance history and a commitment to the INL.

As I was leaving my cubicle, I saw a friend, Dave McGraph. I had always admired Dave for his courage in fighting for the rights of the LGBTQ community and for his service to our country. He had served in the U.S. Army as a captain in Airborne Ranger Military Intelligence. When Dave saw me leaving, he stopped and saluted me. This would always be a very special memory.

A Security staff member escorted me from the second floor of the building to the front entrance. I felt like John Coffey from the movie *The Green Mile* as he walked his final walk to the electric chair.

The two-mile drive home seemed to be in slow motion. As I turned into the neighborhood I thought, *I'm almost there.* I wanted — no, I *needed* to be home. When I opened the door, Lavonna was there waiting for me. We embraced tightly as tears streamed down our faces.

Chapter 69: Life Begins Anew

THE FIRST DAYS of not having a job after thirty-five years were like being in an episode of the *Twilight Zone*. It was real, but at times it didn't feel real. Being home alone while LaVonna was at work was the most difficult time of day. It was a constant struggle trying to understand what had happened and why.

Only one thing was certain and that was I would not give up trying to make a difference. Too many things had been left unfinished. First, BEA had created a culture of fear and intimidation. Employees were reluctant to report issues, which could lead to an unsafe work environment. Second, as Alvarez said, "Diversity is no longer a focus area." The evidence of this was clear. BEA had not recognized Black History Month in 2011 or 2012. And after eight years there was still not a single African American senior manager. Finally, there was not a single African American who worked in the Human Resource division — the division responsible for recruiting and placement of applicants.

With all this in mind, I decided I would write a book about my experiences as a whistleblower. My hope was that doing so would make the INL a better and safer place to work. A place where diversity was valued, as evidenced by greater opportunities for African Americans and other minorities. And finally, I hoped other African Americans wouldn't be subject to discrimination or racism.

I had no idea how to write a book or how to get one published.

Nonetheless, I began the journey with enthusiasm and optimism.

In the meantime I needed to find a job. I believed my thirteen years as an ethics officer and my more recent success working for a senior manager would make me a strong candidate. I believed I would be able to find the right job with the right organization.

However, I also realized there were major obstacles in my path. The full history of my DOE whistleblower case was on the web. If anyone were to Google 'Dennis Patterson INL' or 'Dennis Patterson BEA,' the first thing to pop up would be the DOE Office of Hearing and Appeals report. The report included the names of all the principals involved in the retaliation and, of course, my name. So, I was a fifty-eight-year-old African American who had blown the whistle on the largest employer in the state. Not exactly the profile of a highly marketable job applicant, particularly in Idaho.

Nonetheless, I updated my resume and recruited some very reputable references. On May 21, 2013, I interviewed with Micron Technologies in Boise. The position was 'North American Employee Relations Manager.' LaVonna and I drove to Boise with great expectations. The interview went exceptionally well and I was quite hopeful. In fact, the next day we drove around looking at homes. I was told I would hear back in two weeks.

Unfortunately, three weeks later I had heard nothing. I made several calls, but was unable to reach the recruiter I had been communicating with. Finally, six weeks after the interview a different recruiter called. "Dennis, we have decided to go another direction." This was a phrase I would often hear but never get used to.

Over the next few months, I submitted many applications and had several interviews. Many of them ended with, "We've decided to go another direction." Many never replied. It was increasingly difficult to remain hopeful. But with each rejection, LaVonna would encourage me and remind me that things would work out in the end.

Chapter 70: Black and Blue

ON SEPTEMBER 5, 2013, I read an article in the *Post Register* about an incident involving a Black family and the local police. As I read the story, my emotions went from disappointment to anger to outrage. I thought — not in my city, not in my community. The headline was, "Chief: Race Not a Factor in Tasing." A portion of Ruth Brown's article is below:

A neighbor's noise complaint about a child's birthday party on the 200 block of 18th Street on Saturday night grew into a dispute in which a police officer fired a taser at two men before they were handcuffed and taken to jail.

A series of YouTube videos under the heading, "Cops Out of Control in IF" has drawn more than 1,500 views and raised the allegation that race played a major factor in the arrest.

Idaho Falls Police Chief Mark McBride said race was not a factor in his officers' actions."

"There were no racial comments made in the video until (people at the party) brought it up," McBride said.

A review board determined that the officer who fired the taser was within the bounds of his authority.

Victor Madrigal, 41, was arrested for disturbing the peace, resisting an officer, and battery on an officer. His brother, Delosanto Madrigal, 40, was arrested for disturbing the peace and resisting an officer.

Neighbor Chantal Meek believes racial tensions were a factor in escalating the situation. "I don't see why race wouldn't be an issue with the police. The Madrigals are people who are obviously not from Idaho. I think it was uncalled for."

Meek, who wrote a letter to the Post Register on Tuesday, said two officers barged into her house with their guns drawn Saturday night. She was in her living room studying when the officers came into her house shouting. Meek said she wasn't disturbed by the neighbors' get-together, especially because it was a Saturday night during the summer.

"It was never that invasive and I'm twenty feet from where they were outside," Meek said.

Post Register reporters canvassed the neighborhood Wednesday to talk to people who may have heard the party. None of the neighbors contacted said the party was a disturbance.

In the YouTube video, both the party-goers and the police sounded calm, and quiet laughter could be heard. One of the female party goers said, "It's ok, we'll turn it down."

Shortly thereafter, an officer told Madrigal, the homeowner, that he was going to be given a citation for disturbing the police. Victor Madrigal started swearing about his Idaho neighbors, and an unidentified officer told him, "If you don't like it, you can leave."

Some of the party goers took that to mean Madrigal, a U.S. citizen who immigrated from the Dominican Republic, should move back to his native country.

An officer asked Madrigal for his ID. When Madrigal turned to enter the home — he said he was retrieving his ID — his brother was in the way, according to police reports.

A commotion ensued. In the melee, several police can be seen shoving their way into the house. In the process, they reportedly knocked down a pregnant woman. Idaho Police Department Patrolman Clark Lund fired a taser at both of the Madrigal brothers. Several other officers entered the home with guns drawn. Children and the birthday girl's grandmother were inside at the home.

Within moments, Meeks said, her quiet street was filled with at least eleven police cars.

McBride said his officers acted appropriately in their response to the situation. He said tasers can be used as a method to stop a person from resisting arrest.

The official police department news release said both Madrigal brothers physically resisted the officers, and that Victor Madrigal head-butted an officer during the arrest.

Victor Madrigal said in a phone interview with the Post Register *that he did not fight with the police or try to flee from them.*

Delosanto Madrigal said he was not resisting, but because he and his brother are from Dominican Republic, he thought the officers came there knowing they were going to arrest the men.

"I am a black Hispanic. I think it has to do with my race," Victor Madrigal said. "I have been here in Idaho Falls for a long time. I don't disrespect anybody."

McBride said officers Jessica Marley and Spencer Steel, who walked into Meek's home, will not be disciplined for entering the home uninvited. He called it "an honest mistake" that the dispatch commander will use as a teaching opportunity, "to help them understand the importance of getting (officers) the right address."

Meek said one of the officers did come back and apologize for the mistake.

"From reading the reports, I don't see that officers did anything wrong," McBride said.

The *Post Register* published a follow-up story on February 11, 2014, by Ruth Brown. The following are excerpts from the article:

A jury Friday acquitted an Idaho Falls man of all charges, including battery on an officer, in relation to an altercation at a child's birthday party last summer … after two hours of deliberation, a jury found Victor Manuel Madrigal not guilty.

Idaho Falls Police Department's spokeswoman Joelyn Hansen said the review board's decision is not affected by the jury's verdict and that the issue will not be reviewed again.

Idaho Falls City attorney said officer Eric Rose claimed he was head-butted by Madrigal and that he grabbed the officer's arm.

The jury found otherwise.

Post Register, February 26, 2014, Ali Tadayon:

City Prosecutors dismissed all charges against Victor Delosanto Madrigal.

Post Register, March 2, 2014, Ali Tadayon excerpts:

Members of an Idaho Falls family are demanding a combined $279,500 for damages stemming from an incident at a child's birthday party.

The tort claim seeks reimbursement for property damages and attorney fees as well as compensation. They also demand a public apology from the city of Idaho Falls and Officer Lund, Officer Rose, and Officer Prince for their conduct.

Attorney John Stocish said an apology would go a long way to resolve some of the damages sought in the tort claim.

Police Chief McBride said his department has no plans to apologize. 'I don't know why there would be an apology. Just because a person is found not guilty doesn't mean the officers were wrong.'

Post Register, March 18, 2016, Tom Holm excerpt:

In Manuel Madrigal's trial, Officer Rose admitted under oath that he 'fudged' information in the incident report pertaining to Manuel Madrigal allegedly grabbing his arm and headbutting him.

'Everything was kind of a blur that night,' Rose said in court. 'My adrenalin was pumping the whole night after an event like that and I remembered the main events that happened. I fudged the sequence of how they happened, though … they were wrong.'

***

As a former ethics officer who had conducted hundreds of investigations and advised senior managers on ethical issues, I was deeply troubled by the actions of the police officers, the 'review board' and the police chief.

In my opinion the first mistake was the officers asking for Madrigal's driver's license. If a police officer came to my home based on a noise complaint and asked for my license, I would refuse to give it to them. This appeared to be the event that triggered all the subsequent events. I'm not convinced the officer would have asked for the license if Madrigal was white. I'm also not convinced that race wasn't a factor in the tasing.

The most egregious act was the officer who 'fudged' the incident report. Nothing in the news report suggested that the officer received any discipline, and apparently the review board took no further action.

With respect to the review board, it is my understanding that the board included at least two police officers. In my opinion the results were predictable. It is difficult for police officers to provide an unbiased assessment of their brothers in uniform. In my opinion there should be a citizens' review board, independent from the police department.

Chief McBride's apparent unwillingness to entertain the possibility his officers could have done anything wrong is unfortunate. Finally, it is my experience that an apology can go a long way in resolving conflict and building bridges. From the whole debacle only one officer apologized, and that apology was to the white person next door.

I hope the police department and/or the city learned from this event and put in place policies and procedures to improve the interaction between citizens and police officers.

Chapter 71: Mixed Blessings

THE THEME FOR THE 2014 DR. KING BANQUET was 'The Power of Hope.' The keynote speaker was our own Dr. Lucretia Murphy. Lucretia arrived with her parents in Idaho Falls when she was a young child in the early 1970s. She excelled scholastically, was Idaho's 1988 Junior Miss, and third runner-up in America's Junior Miss competition. Lucretia went on to earn a law degree and a Ph.D. in higher education policy.

The banquet room was filled to capacity. Lucretia opened her talk by giving honor to her parents — "my mom (Shirley) was the best teacher at Idaho Falls High School." She noted that her father (Llew) had been a chemist at the Idaho National Laboratory and one-time president of the local NAACP.

Giving tribute to Dr. King she said, "I believe and affirm that Martin Luther King was an American hero who helped the nation realize its better ideals and helped all of us realize our better selves."

Dr. Murphy encouraged all of us to "remember who you are and where you came from." Another statement she made still rings in my ears: "The power of hope helps people in the pit of darkness keep going."

When I was in the pit for almost four years, I never lost hope. At the close of her talk the audience gave her a standing ovation.

As always, the proceeds were used to donate to a local charity and provide scholarships. One of the recipients was Ibukun Omatowa. The following fall he would attend Harvard University. He later graduated with degrees in molecular biology and history. The African American Alliance was proud to play a small role in this amazing achievement.

***

On March 25, 2014, I had the honor and privilege to be an invited speaker at the National Association of Employee Concerns Program in San Francisco, California. I spoke about my experience being a DOE whistleblower. Many of the attendees expressed disbelief that a government contractor would take such actions against any employee, let alone the ethics officer. The highlight of the trip was when LaVonna and I had lunch with Billie Garde. For most of the lunch we talked about the wonderments of life, kids, grandkids, and such. But inevitably, the subject turned to our respective tragic whistleblower journeys. At the end of lunch, we hugged and wished each other well.

***

On March 28, 2014 DOE announced that it had extended BEA's contract to operate and manage the INL. The DOE said the decision was based on BEA's 'proven performance and success' in managing the site. Members of Idaho's congressional delegation issued a press release: "Bea's Extension at INL Well-Deserved." Most of the employees I spoke to were very disheartened and disappointed, but no one seemed surprised.

***

Pulitzer Prize winner Isabel Wilkerson visited Idaho Falls on April 17, 2014. She was the author of the national best seller, *The Warmth of Other Suns*. The book chronicled the epic migration of almost six million Blacks who fled the South for northern and western cities in search of a better life. The Idaho Humanities Council had invited her as part of their annual distinguished lecture program. An informal meet-and-greet was held at the home of Anne Voilleque.

Anne had been one of the largest contributors to my 2007 campaign for city council.

LaVonna and I had the pleasure of getting to know Ms. Wilkerson. She was amazingly gracious, but also down to earth. I shared a brief synopsis of my upcoming book, *Whistleblower*. When she autographed a copy of her book for me, she wrote, "To Dennis and LaVonna, best of luck with your new book." It was quite an honor.

Chapter 72: The Release

AFTER MORE THAN A YEAR spending hundreds of hours writing my first book, it was now ready for release. On May 25, 2014, my editor and friend, Michael Strickland, officially launched, *Whistleblower: Justice Over Discrimination and Ethics Violations.* The cover prominently displayed the DOE and INL logos. My good friend Kurt Hamman assisted with the design.

The launching of the book was my first step in my ongoing effort to make the INL a better place. It was also my way of giving hope to others. If I could make a difference for even one person, it would be worth all the pain, struggle, and sacrifice.

***

June 14, 2014, was a very special day. I was honored to be presented the 2014 Loving Day Celebration and Progressive Award. The celebration was established to commemorate the Supreme Court decision that struck down the laws forbidding interracial marriage. The framed certificate read: "In Grateful Recognition, this Progressive Award is Given to Dennis Patterson for being a beacon of light in our community, for displaying great moral courage, and for demonstrating the true meaning of equality and justice."

The award was presented by Dan Henry, chapter host for the Idaho Falls Chapter of Drinking Liberally. This organization promoted inclusive progressive conversations in Idaho Falls and surrounding areas.

On June 17 I applied for a position with the Idaho Human Rights Commission. I never heard back. I suspected they 'decided to go another direction.'

On August 11 I sent an email to Brenda Jones, Office of US Representative John Lewis: "The Idaho Falls African American Alliance would love to have Congressman Lewis be our keynote speaker for our 2015 Dr. King banquet. It would be a defining and historical experience for our community and our state." Unfortunately, we were later informed that John Lewis would be unable to attend.

Late in August the Intermountain Energy Summit convened here in Idaho Falls. In attendance was DOE Energy Secretary Earnest Moniz. I took the opportunity to deliver a hardcopy of my book to Moniz. I handed it to Ivy Berry, CFO of the *Post Register*. He assured me he would get it to Moniz. I believed the power of truth and transparency would lead to positive changes at the INL. The book was now in the hands of someone who could make those changes.

My next promising interview was the end of August with Boise State University for an employee relations position. I believed the interview had gone well and that LaVonna and I might soon be moving to Boise. Unfortunately, two months later I received the dreaded news. They had decided to go another direction.

My first ever book signing was held on September 27, 2014, at the Idaho Falls Barnes & Nobles. The experience was overwhelming as people formed a long line to buy an autographed copy of *Whistleblower*. I enjoyed catching up with some of my INL colleagues and meeting new people who would later become friends. LaVonna stood by with her beautiful smile. It was a day to remember.

In early November the *Post Register* published an article announcing the replacement of John Grossenbacher. The article referenced many successes but also referenced my successful whistleblower complaint.

On November 23 I sent an email to Mayor Casper and the city council. I referenced my book and suggested they read chapters 51 and 52 which detailed a whistleblower complaint filed against the city in the 90s by city engineer Ed Turner. I encouraged them to read and learn from the past.

Mayor Casper responded the next day. "I have read the recommended chapters. I appreciate your experience and integrity." Her response was a powerful example of a leader willing to learn from the past.

On December 9 I received the following email from Congressman Mike Simpson: "Thank you for your message regarding the book you wrote about your time at the INL. I have reviewed your comments as have my staff and I will keep them in mind as I make decisions that affect Idaho and its citizens."

On December 14 the Pocatello newspaper, *Idaho State Journal,* published a front-page story, "INL Whistleblower Alleges Violations at the Site." Included in the article was a response from BEA: "Spokeswoman Amy Lentz said last week that the company has no comment regarding Patterson's book. We haven't bought the book and we don't intend to."

This comment from BEA did not surprise me. It was a continuance of BEA's unwillingness to learn from the past and accept responsibility for its actions.

Further, in my mind it was also an effort to show disdain and disrespect toward me. I had heard that BEA was openly discouraging employees and managers from reading the book.

Chapter 73: 2015 Great ... and Then ...

AT THE BEGINNING OF 2015, I began my post INL career. I decided to become a substitute teacher. I loved engaging with students. I had the opportunity not only to educate, but to influence the lives of young people. Many students had never seen a teacher of color.

It wasn't uncommon for Hispanic and Black students to talk to me after class or during lunch. I was able to provide encouragement and hope for all the students, but especially for those from disadvantaged backgrounds.

One of the great joys of teaching was having fun with the students. I loved messing with them. On occasion I would tell them that President Obama was my cousin and he was coming to school to speak to them. Most of the time they believed me.

***

I extended an invitation to Idaho Falls Mayor Rebecca Casper to welcome guests at the upcoming 2015 Dr. Martin Luther King banquet. She graciously accepted.

The MC for the event was Jolyn Thomas, local radio host and member of the Idaho Falls African American Alliance. During her introduction, she informed the audience that the proceeds from the banquet and silent auction would support scholarships and a local charity. She added, "One of the items I'd like to highlight is a book, *Whistleblower*, donated by author Dennis Patterson. It is a brilliant book. He does a great job of connecting the dots, providing insight, and sharing valuable life lessons." I sat there wondering if any of the BEA senior managers present might be interested in bidding on the book. Probably not.

I had the honor of introducing the keynote speaker, the honorable Cherie-Buckner Webb. She spoke powerfully and eloquently. She began, "We pause to honor those who made a way for us, to acknowledge their achievements. To celebrate their perseverance. We have come a mighty long way. I stand before you to say to you, in the vernacular, "We ain't done yet. The battle is not yet won, inaction is not an option. I ask each of you what is in your arsenal to combat the injustices that permeate our society, the sexism the racism, the homophobia, the geographic privilege and more.

"We have a responsibility to leave a legacy, tell the stories, make the history of struggle and accomplishment real for the next generation."

Cherie spoke about the need to stand up for something you believe in, to speak up, and find your voice. And to look up, to call on that power greater than yourself.

In closing she joked about a time when President Obama visited Boise State University. People asked her if she was going to get to meet him. She responded by telling them that he was her cousin. She laughed about how many people believed her. She told us she did actually get to meet him. When she was introduced to him, she whispered, "Yes, there are Black people in Idaho. And he responded, "I just doubled the population when I came."

Cherie's keynote address resonated throughout the banquet. Her words were authentic, inspirational, and hopeful. I was proud to know that African Americans in Idaho had such powerful representation, not just in the legislature but throughout the state and the nation.

***

March 18, 2015, I was an invited speaker at the Annual Ethics and Compliance Conference in Austin, Texas. It was an honor and privilege to share my story with ethics professionals from around the world.

The program for the conference included the following: "Journey from Ethics Officer to Whistleblower." The program description said: "In preparing for a new day in ethics and compliance, we must learn from history. This is a first-person account of a seasoned ethics officer and former member of this organization who fought for fairness and justice at our nation's lead nuclear research facility, the Idaho National Laboratory. He will powerfully describe the threats, intimidation, and harassment he endured and finally, after four years, how he was vindicated when a hearing officer ruled in his favor."

It was more than ironic that the world's premiere ethics organization chose to learn from history, yet INL's public statement was that it had no intention to even read the book.

***

On April 16, 2015, Pulitzer Prize winning author Diane McWhorton visited Idaho Falls as a speaker for the Idaho Humanities Council. She was the author of *Carry Me Home,* a book about the Civil Rights struggle in Birmingham, Alabama. LaVonna and I had the opportunity to visit with her after her keynote address. I shared with her my story as a whistleblower. She was kind enough to do me a special favor. She allowed for a picture to be taken with her holding my book and me holding her book. It was quite an honor.

***

Mark Peters took over as Laboratory Director for the INL on October 1, 2015. Two weeks later, I sent Peters an email. "I respectfully ask that you read my book, *Whistleblower: Justice over Discrimination and Ethics Violations.* Although I never received a response from Peters, I was hopeful that he bought and read my book.

Later in October, I applied for what appeared to be a job ideally suited to my experience as an ethics officer. The job title was 'Advisor Ethics and Compliance Specialist.' Shortly thereafter, I participated in a telephone interview with the director of the organization. He lived back east but was responsible for the position here in Idaho Falls. If there was ever a perfect interview, this was it. He called me the next day and told me I would have an in-person interview on November 12 in Idaho Falls at the Bechtel Bettis Naval Reaction Facility.

The morning of the interview I was prepared, dressed, and ready to go. Then my cell phone rang.

"Dennis, I needed to call you and tell you the job has been cancelled because of budget issues."

I had been disappointed many times before, but nothing like this. How could this be? LaVonna overheard the call. She put her arms around me. There was nothing to be said. I didn't believe the excuse about budget issues. In my opinion, the real reason had more to do with my being a whistleblower.

Within a few days, there was a disappointment of a different kind. I learned that Mark Olsen had returned to the INL as General Counsel for BEA. Not only that, but it was my information that he would have oversight of the BEA Ethics Office. The words, 'white privilege' echoed in my head. In my opinion and experience, an African American would never be given the chance to return to the same job after losing a high-profile whistleblower case. But just as Benson returned from his time at Battelle corporate, Olsen was now back.

Chapter 74: Good, Bad, and Sad

JUNE 2016 BEA announced it had hired Zachary Tudor as Associate Laboratory Director for National Homeland Security. For the first time in the past sixteen years there was an African American in senior leadership of the INL. Zach later told me that he accepted the position, in part, for the opportunity to be a mentor and role model for African Americans.

***

At the INL, more positive changes were occurring. On October 27, 2016, the following news release was issued: "We welcome Toni Carter — Inclusion and Diversity Lead — who will oversee efforts to augment an inclusive work culture for the entire laboratory." Toni was an African American female. Only three years ago, Alvarez had said diversity was not a focus area for Battelle.

Whatever the reason for this change, I was hopeful this would result in more opportunities for African Americans and other minorities. And perhaps a greater appreciation for the value of all employees.

Also, in October a community forum to discuss racial injustice was held at the Unitarian Universalist Church. The meeting was prompted by the vandalizing of a Black Lives Matter banner that was posted outside the church. The banner had been posted in response to high-profile police shootings of African Americans around the nation. The forum was hosted by Reverend Lyn Stangland Cameron.

I had become good friends with Lyn over the past several years. She had an amazing passion for fairness, justice, and equality.

The forum was attended by approximately eighty community members, including Mayor Rebecca Casper. Both Casper and I spoke. While our experiences and perspectives were different, we had an open and constructive dialogue. For me, this was an example of great leadership.

The forum affirmed my belief that the power of dialogue can lead to positive outcomes. I was hopeful that my community would learn from the past, recognize the present challenges, and work toward a better future.

***

On November 8, 2016, I experienced the exact opposite emotions from those I experienced on November 4, 2008. Instead of hope, joy, and elation, I felt overwhelming despair, sadness, and depression. To my horror, Donald Trump had been elected president of the United States. A man who rose to political prominence with racist birtherism claims about Obama and derogatory remarks about Mexicans and Muslims was now our country's leader. It was one of the most difficult days of my life. Nonetheless, it would not keep me from believing in the goodness of America. The struggle had just gotten harder.

***

The annual Dr. King banquet was held on January 19, 2017. The keynote speaker was Eric Love. Eric had served as the first African American student body president at Boise State University. He was the director of staff diversity and inclusion at Notre Dame University.

Eric spoke passionately about his commitment to social justice. He informed us that one of his proudest achievements was his role in having the state of Idaho recognize the Dr. Martin Luther Jr. holiday. He testified before the Idaho legislature. In spring of 1990 the legislature passed the Martin Luther King Jr. Idaho Human Rights Day. He told us that during the bill signing ceremony, Idaho Governor Cecil Andrus said, "There is one person who without his work this would not have happened, and that is Eric Love."

For me these were exceedingly powerful words. It was a demonstration that one person really can make a difference.

In his closing remarks, he said, "I have a suggestion. I think a Dr. Martin Luther King Boulevard would look awesome in Idaho Falls." Most in the audience applauded. I hoped the applause included city leadership and the senior leaders of the INL who were present. I now had a dream that one day Idaho Falls would honor Dr. King by naming a street after him.

***

Jamaica's diverse ethnic roots are reflected in its national motto: "Out of Many One People." Jamaica is a beautiful island with beautiful Black people. It is a place I had always wanted to experience. On February 28, 2017, LaVonna and I landed in Montego Bay for a five-day vacation of wonderment. We spent a lot of time on the pristine white sandy beaches with the crystal blue water. For adventure, we climbed the famed 180-foot high Dunn River Falls. As we made our way to the top we stopped to play in lush surroundings and pools.

The most amazing part of the trip was getting to know some of the native islanders. It was fascinating to hear the stories of family and island history.

I was enthralled with the music, dancing, and rhythmic drums. LaVonna and I immersed ourselves in a place we had only dreamed of as little kids in small towns in North Carolina and Idaho.

In early March 2017 my brother, Pastor Patterson, was diagnosed with cancer. This was devastating to his wife as well as the rest of the family. He soon began treatments and as a result he was often unable to preach Sunday morning sermons.

During this time, he became friends with Apostle Gary Carter from Chicago, Illinois. Carter filled in for my brother as needed. March 29 was my brother's 69th birthday. There was a birthday party in the church fellowship hall. Most of the family was present.

At a pause in the celebration, Apostle Carter said he had something to say. He began by stating, "Dennis has paved the way for many African Americas at the INL." He went on to make other complimentary remarks about me. While I wasn't certain of his sincerity, it was the first time I had heard anyone with ties to the INL acknowledge anything positive about my contribution to the INL. It felt good.

My brother passed on August 25, 2017. He had pastored for twenty-four years. Death is always hard to understand and the pain resides deep within. But our family pulled together and helped each other make it through. His wife, Euranius, and the rest of us were proud of the legacy he left behind. A legacy of love, compassion, commitment, and faith.

Chapter 75: A Second Chance

THIS WAS MY FOURTH YEAR SUBSTITUTE TEACHING. I had been subbing for all grades K–12 and most days I thoroughly enjoyed what I was doing. May 23, 2018, was not one of those days. When I arrived at work, I wasn't feeling the best. My teaching assignment was a fourth-grade class on the second floor. When I got to the top of the stairs that morning, I felt a little winded, but didn't pay it much attention. It only took a few minutes in front of the class to realize that today was going to be a very long day. A few kids exhibited serious behavior issues. They would speak out of turn, get out of their seats, and were generally disruptive.

I used all my training and experience to manage the classroom but nothing seemed to work. By lunch time I was wondering if I was going to make it through the day. As the day wound to a close, I was certain I didn't want to substitute for elementary grades any more. I walked the students downstairs and out to their bus. When I got to the top of the stairs, I had to pause to catch my breath. I took a few steps inside the classroom.

The next thing I remember was lying on the floor with the back of my head bleeding. Although disoriented, I got to my feet and made it to my desk. I finished up my paperwork, walked down the stairs, and out to my car. I thought if I could just make it home everything would be alright. As I drove past Pine Creek Golf Course, I realized it was a bad idea to be driving. I called LaVonna and told her what had happened.

We met and she drove me to the hospital. We soon had the diagnosis — it was a heart attack and I needed surgery. The next morning, I had three stents put into my arteries. My doctor told me one of the arteries was 99 percent blocked.

I was released from the hospital the next day. After five days of light restrictions, I was able to resume normal activities. The realization that I could have died right there in the classroom didn't hit me until several days later. That's when I began to do some self-reflection and introspection. I wasn't sure what my future would look like, but I was certain there was much left for me to do. God had given me a second chance and I was going to make the most of it.

***

In June Jasmine informed LaVonna and me that she and her fiancé, Chance Gilbert, were ready to get married and they wanted to be married on July 1. With only weeks to plan the ceremony we booked the Hilton Garden Inn, made all the family and friend notifications, and were ready on schedule. It was a gorgeous day, almost perfect for an outdoor wedding. Jasmine looked beautiful in her stunning white gown. I was so proud and so happy as she took my arm and I walked her down the aisle. This was a moment I had looked forward to ever since she was a little girl. I was so thankful that God had blessed me to see this day.

***

In January 2019 I happened to be reading an article in the Boise newspaper, the *Idaho Statesman*. It was if I was reading my own thoughts.

Idaho Statesman January 25, 2019 by Adam Schasel, 'Guest Opinion.'

It's been nearly thirty years, can we simply call it Martin Luther Jr. Day.

It's no secret that Idaho was not always Martin Luther King Jr's biggest fan.

Idaho was the 47th state to officially recognize the holiday, seven years after President Ronald Reagan signed a bill creating a federal MLK. Even then, Idaho Lawmakers were less than enthusiastic about the idea — having previously rejecting it in 1986 — citing cost concerns or King's perceived irrelevance to Idaho. Some legislators attacked King's character, citing his infidelities or alleging that he had pro-Russian sympathies. But the desire to shed a national association with white supremacy and the Aryan Nation finally pushed reluctant lawmakers to compromise with their more forward thinking colleagues and recognize the third Monday of January as Martin Luther King Jr. — Human Rights Day.

I guess the name could have been worse. We could be Alabama or Mississippi, where King shares his holiday with Confederate General Robert E. Lee.

Certainly, wanting a holiday to celebrate the advancement, sanctity, and universality of human rights is a laudable goal. But combining MLK Day with a generic, feel-good holiday for human rights mimics the same reasons that it is tone-deaf to say All Lives Matter. Of course, all lives matter, but in America, Black lives often get valued less in important ways. Given the distinct, lasting legacy of American slavery and white supremacy, I think it's fair to spread some love around the calendar.

Idaho has a long way to go on the path of true equality. But the first step is easy – we should just call it Martin Luther King Jr. Day. The idea of King being a controversial figure was laughable in 1990. Twenty-nine years later, it's just insulting.

Adam Schasel's eloquent writing resonated in the deepest part of my soul. I had always been disappointed that Idaho had never given Dr. King the honor and respect he deserved. I was now hopeful that would change some day.

***

I could never pass up the opportunity to speak out whenever I heard or read about racial issues in Idaho Falls.

In the summer of 2019 Representative Barbara Ehardt, an Idaho Republican lawmaker from Idaho Falls, wrote a letter to Boise State University President Marlene Tromp criticizing the school's diversity efforts. Three other Republican lawmakers signed the letter. The letter was critical of scholarships available for students of diverse backgrounds and funding to promote inclusiveness and cultural awareness.

After reading several articles and commentaries in the newspaper, I became convinced that I needed to communicate my thoughts to Ehardt. Because we already knew each other, I chose to engage with her via Facebook. I challenged her position that diversity programs were not needed and that such programs weren't fair to white people. I shared with her my personal experience and offered my opinion that white privilege is real and thus we need diversity programs.

Of course, I didn't change her mind. But I was glad I tried to influence her thinking on this very important subject. I believed that Ehardt had no understanding, compassion, or empathy for the victims of discrimination, racism, and injustice.

***

As fall approached LaVonna and I were wondering which bucket list we would check off this year. Over the recent years we had gone on cruises, visited Jamaica, London, and Paris.

We decided we would go on the 'Faith and Family Caribbean Cruise with T. D. Jakes.' The spiritual experience was amazing. Bishop Jakes gave uplifting messages and the music was awesome. The highlight was the beautiful sounds of renowned gospel singers Kenny Lattimore and Jonathan Butler.

Culturally, I enjoyed being immersed in the African American experience. Of the more than two thousand cruisers, approximately 95 percent of us were Black, including our niece Donne' and her mom, Euranius. Whenever LaVonna and I introduced ourselves and where we were from, the most common response was, "I didn't know there were Black people in Idaho." Other responses included, "I have friends who live in Des Moines," and "Oh yeah, you guys have those famous potatoes." All such comments were said and received in good humor. We made several new friends, some of whom will be part of our lives.

In the fall of 2019 LaVonna and I decided to invite all our adult children and grandchildren to spend Christmas with us. The highlight would be going snow machining in the great outdoors of Island Park, Idaho. Although I was a native of Idaho, I had never been a great outdoorsman.

The North Carolina gang included our daughter Valderia (Emanuel), their fifteen-year-old son Isaiah, and Trish; Jasmine (Chance), and their kids Janessa and Jayden (their daughter Azlynn couldn't make it) came from Boise.

The day after Christmas was perfect. The sun was shining, blue skies, and brisk temperatures. We all had on our rented gear, gloves, and helmets. Chance had grown up in Rigby, Idaho and was an experienced snow machiner. The rest of us looked good but had no idea what we were doing.

Nonetheless, we had an experience to remember. LaVonna was driving while I rode on the back. She inadvertently gunned the throttle and we both went flying through the air. Fortunately we landed in soft powdery snow. The only thing bruised was our egos. At the end of the day, Isaiah drove one of the machines back to the rental place, with me on the back. As directed by his mom, I tried to keep him from going too fast. Well, that didn't work. I hung on for dear life and prayed all the way back.

Our vacation could only have been better if the whole family could have made it. Maybe next time.

Chapter 76: The Year of 2020

THE BEGINNING OF 2020 WAS AWESOME. The keynote speaker for the Dr. King banquet was Julius Caesar (J.C.) Watts. J. C. had been a college football hero and an Oklahoma Republican Congressman. Now, Watts was about to launch the "Black News Channel," a venue to give the African American community a voice.

In his address Watts stated, "Dr. King was the conscience of the nation because he knew that every single person on the face of the earth — red, yellow, brown, black or white, man or woman — had worth because of their creator."

Watts continued, "In spite of the fact that I might disagree with you, your life is no less valuable. The fact that you might disagree with others, their lives are no less sacred."

The crowd enjoyed his keynote address immensely. It was a timely and important message. For the past three years our country had become more divisive and more hateful. Too many people had forgotten about the sanctity and dignity of life. But in Idaho Falls we were being reminded that we are all in this together and we all have God-given worth.

***

Jasmine called and told me she would be going back to college. She was going to pursue a degree in law.

"Awesome, Jazz; why law?" I said.

"Because I have always had a passion for helping others. I want to be the voice for those who aren't being heard. I want to fight against the injustices many Americans face every day. I want to make the world a better place, even if it is one battle at a time."

For her English writing class Jasmine produced a podcast titled, "Racism in Idaho." She interviewed me and Charles Taylor, president of the Boise chapter of the National Association for the Advancement of Colored People.

I was so very proud of Jasmine and so hopeful for her future and that of her family.

***

I was now completing my fifth year of substitute teaching. I felt blessed to be making a difference in the lives of young people. During any given week I had the opportunity to teach up to 750 students. When time allowed, we discussed issues ranging from their responsibility to speak up if they saw bullying to reporting abuse from adults. A few years before a substitute teacher had been sent to prison for sexually abusing a couple of middle school students at his home.

We also discussed the importance of diversity and respecting each other regardless of race, creed, color, or religion. During Black History month, I would ask what they knew. More often than not, they knew very little. Most only knew about Dr. King and Rosa Parks. I hoped that one day the local schools would do a better job of teaching children about the great contributions of the many African Americans who helped make America the great nation that it is.

***

In mid-March all schools were shut down because of the Coronavirus. While I missed the kids, the time gave me the opportunity to relax and spend more time with my beautiful wife. She was keeping busy writing her first novel, *The House on the Dirty*

Road. As a result of our many conversations, she inspired me to write a second book. I had no idea what the title would be, but I immediately knew what the subject would be.

***

On May 26, 2020, George Floyd, a forty-six-year-old Black man was killed in Minneapolis, Minnesota. Floyd was handcuffed, lying face down, and begging for his life. A white police officer had his knee on Floyd's neck for eight minutes and forty-six seconds.

The horrific murder of Floyd brought to light the issue of police brutality, institutional racism, legal injustice, and white privilege. Protests erupted across America, even in Idaho Falls.

Beginning shortly after George's murder, Black Lives Matter demonstrations were held weekly at the Broadway Bridge overlooking the Snake River. I was proud to see the number of young people and people of all colors protesting with signs and chanting, "Black Lives Matter." LaVonna and I joined on several occasions. Of course, there were times when we got flipped off and heard the N word, but that was nothing compared to the many horn honks and thumbs up. The demonstrations continued throughout the summer.

Down the street from the demonstrations was the restaurant which in 1993 had displayed the paintings of local artist Werner Gisin. At that time, Gisin had made public racist comments about Blacks and Mexicans when an affordable housing development was being proposed.

I stopped by the restaurant for lunch to see if the paintings were still on display. As I walked in I could see them. I was seated at a booth. I noticed there were only two other tables with patrons. The server seemed to see me, but didn't bother to come take my order. I sat there for about fifteen minutes without being served. When a white couple came in she immediately went over and took their order.

I waited until she finished. I walked over and quietly said, "It would have been nice if you had served me first." She just looked at me and walked away. Feeling angry and hurt, I decided to leave. On my way out I mentioned this to the three employees at the front counter. One of them responded, "Maybe she didn't see you." The subject server overheard the comment and stated, "No, I saw him, but I thought I'd serve them first and then work my way down to him."

While I can't be certain that this incident was racist or even discriminatory, I know how it made me feel, and likely how any person of color would feel under the same circumstances.

On June 20 hundreds of people marched from the Museum of Idaho to the pavilion along the Snake River. The theme of the march was Standing Together. I was so incredibly proud as LaVonna and I — along with family and friends — participated in one of the largest marches in the history of Idaho Falls. I was honored to be one of the speakers, along with Mayor Rebecca Casper; Police Chief Bryce Johnson; city councilman Jim Francis; INL director of inclusion, Toni Carter; and Jeremy Herman, president of Citizens for Accountability, Advocacy and Public Safety (CAAPS).

I concluded my remarks with the following: "2016 was the year Colin Kaepernick kneeled during the national anthem to protest against racial injustice, police brutality, and systemic oppression. Maybe if our nation, our communities, our churches had recognized that Black Lives Matter, and that it was okay to protest peacefully by kneeling, maybe Breonna Taylor would not have been killed in her own apartment.

Maybe George Floyd wouldn't have had a knee on his neck for over eight minutes.

And maybe a Black man wouldn't have been shot in the back just a few days ago."

I had joined CAAPS in early June after an article in the *Post*

Register. CAAP's objective was to work with city leadership to identify institutional racism and bias that lead to worse outcomes for Blacks and other people of color. And to take action to eliminate and/or mitigate the outcomes. A special area of emphasis was the police department. A primary objective was to establish a citizen review board to oversee police activities related to incidents involving the use of force. CAAPS also advocates for mental health crisis intervention training, clear requirements for use of force, revoking the doctrine of qualified immunity, and banning 'no-knock' warrants.

At the request of Dave Snell and Pat Tucker, Chairwoman of Bonneville Democrats, I wrote a commentary published in the *Post Register.* The title was, "Now, let's have the conversation about racism." In the article I shared my opinion that institutional racism exists in our nation and in Idaho Falls. I closed that article with, "It is my hope that our community is ready to learn about our history with racism as it works together to build a better future."

***

In July I was in communication with a friend, LaDonna Foster. She had been the vice president of the African American Alliance (AAA) when it was formed in 2006. At the time she had been the Department of Energy Idaho, African American Opportunity Special Emphasis Program Manager.

LaDonna told me that around the time we formed the AAA, she had filed a discrimination complaint against DOE–ID with DOE Headquarters in Washington D.C. She had alleged that her being African American led to her being passed over for promotional opportunities. LaDonna said what bothered her the most was that she had four degrees, including two masters, yet DOE–ID would choose less qualified white individuals. In some cases even those who didn't meet the basic requirements.

I couldn't help but see the irony of her having the position she had, yet she ended up filing a racial discrimination complaint. It was not unlike me being the ethics officer and accusing BEA of misconduct. According to LaDonna the resolution to her case was 'an undisclosed settlement.' She noted that she had retired several years previously.

In my opinion, the settlement was DOE–Idaho's way of making the complaint go away. To my knowledge, in the seventy-one-year history of DOE Idaho, there had only been one African American in senior management. To me, this did not demonstrate a commitment to diversity.

Within a few weeks of my communication with LaDonna I was contacted via LinkedIn. The person informed me she was African American and had been terminated by BEA in the spring. The facts she shared were very similar to my experience. She had been investigated by security and her performance had been questioned. The big difference is that she was terminated within a short time. She said she believed she had been treated differently than her white colleagues and provided an example. A white female in human resources had been promoted to a deputy manager position. Allegedly this person only had a high school diploma. The caller told me that by contrast she had a master's degree. I shared some information about my experience and suggested she read my book. I wished her well.

I didn't know the veracity of her statements but it disappointed me that BEA may not have learned from their past experiences with African Americans.

***

On August 11 Democratic presidential nominee Joe Biden named Kamala Harris as his running mate, making the California senator the first Black and South Asian American to run on a major political party's presidential ticket. It was a very proud moment for millions of Americans, but especially so for the Patterson family.

August 28 was a historic diversity moment for Idaho Falls. KIFI Local News 8 announced that Bre Clark would become the main news anchor. With that, Idaho had its first African American news anchor. A few years earlier Bre and her husband, Tyler, had become good friends with us. We were all very proud of her.

***

Over the past three years Darius received two promotions and now was a manager at one of the Boise Fred Meyer retail stores. In August, he was selected to be one of the African Americans in the corporation to participate in discussions about race and diversity. The discussions would include the president of Fred Meyer and other senior leaders. To me, this was a great example of corporate responsibility. LaVonna and I were proud of Darius for accepting the opportunity to have a voice in promoting diversity.

***

Horrifically, in September Trump's administration issued a directive that prohibited agencies from using federal funds to administer diversity and anti-discrimination training. In the executive memo issued by the Office of Management and Budget, director Russell Vought claimed that diversity trainings "run counter to the fundamental beliefs for which our nation has stood since its inception" and also "engender division and resentment within the federal workforce."

This action led the Department of Energy to direct all National Laboratories to suspend their diversity, equity, and inclusion training programs. As a result the INL suspended all such programs.

It sickened me that 45 would take such an egregious action at a time when America was faced with police brutality, racial injustice, and racial oppression. Our nation needed more understanding of our racial, ethnic, cultural, and lifestyle differences ... not less.

***

I had the honor of writing a commentary in the *Post Register* to recognize the passing of my hero, John Lewis, titled, "Tribute to

John Lewis, an American Hero." I shared a quote from a speech he had given at a college commencement address in 2014.

In the final analysis, we must all learn to live together. As brothers and sisters, we all live in the same house, and it doesn't matter if we are Black or White, Latino, Asian American, or Native American. It doesn't matter if you are straight or gay. We are one people, one family, we all live in the same house. Be bold, be courageous, stand up, speak up, speak out, and find a way to create the beloved world, the world of peace, we are one people, and one love.

These words provide a beacon of light that if followed will make each of us better, but more importantly will make us a better people. We must do this for ourselves, our children, and the generations of grandchildren. I will never stop fighting for fairness, justice, and equality. Neither should you.

Made in the USA
Coppell, TX
16 December 2021

69021989R00154